A BIOFEEDBACK PRIMER

A BIOFEEDBACK PRIMER

Edward B. Blanchard
SUNY AT ALBANY

Leonard H. Epstein
AUBURN UNIVERSITY

ADDISON-WESLEY
PUBLISHING COMPANY

Reading, Massachusetts
Menlo Park, California
London • Amsterdam
Don Mills, Ontario • Sydney

This book is in the
ADDISON-WESLEY SERIES
IN CLINICAL AND PROFESSIONAL
PSYCHOLOGY

Leonard D. Goodstein
Series Editor

 Printed in the United States of America. Published simultaneously in Canada. Library of Congress Catalog Card No. 77-074321.

ISBN 0-201-00338-4
BCDEFGHIJK-DO-798

Foreword

Clinical psychology is a rapidly expanding area of inquiry and practice. Traditional lines between clinical and the other subdisciplines of psychology are rapidly eroding. Research in information processing has direct impact upon behavior therapy, work in physiological psychology affects our work in biofeedback, community psychologists need to keep abreast of what is happening in social psychology, and so on. At the same time, clinical psychologists are being called on to work in a variety of new settings, and to continually develop new skills as well as utilize their existing skills. Health Maintenance organizations (HMOs) ask clinical psychologists not only to provide direct clinical service to clients but also to help change the health-related behaviors of clients who do not require direct service. Community mental health centers ask their clinicians to provide direct service and to assist in developing prevention programs and program evaluation procedures. These are but a few examples of how the field of clinical psychology is expanding.

It is difficult for the professional practitioner as well as the student of clinical psychology to keep in touch with what is happening in the field. Traditional textbooks can give only superficial coverage to these recent changes and the journal literature does not provide a broad overview. The Addison-Wesley Series in Clinical and Professional Psychology is an effort to fill this gap. Taken as a whole, the series could be used as an introduction to the field of clinical psychology. A subset of these books, such as those on therapy, for example, could serve as a text for a course in therapy. Single volumes can be used for seminars when supplemented by journal articles, or as supplemental texts for courses in which the instructor feels the text is lacking in coverage of that area, or for short courses for the active professional. We hope that each of these volumes, written or edited by an expert in the area, will also serve as an up-to-date overview of that area for the interested professional who feels in need of updating.

In this volume Edward B. Blanchard and Leonard H. Epstein present a comprehensive analysis of what we now know about biofeedback. Beginning with the conceptual problems inherent in this emerging field, they present a thorough and incisive analysis of the research literature, one that can serve both as an introduction to the field and as a review to those whose knowledge is scattered or fragmentary.

Webster defines a *primer* as a small introductory volume on a subject. Blanchard and Epstein have produced such a primer, and a highly readable one at that.

Leonard D. Goodstein

Acknowledgments

The authors would like to thank the following people for their assistance in various phases of the preparation of this book: for invaluable assistance in typing the several drafts of the manuscripts we would like to thank Sharon Cross and Debbie Moore; for proofreading and much assistance in making the manuscript readable and it is hoped, understandable, we wish to thank Cris Blanchard and Lynn Parker; and for stimulation and collaboration in much of our own research in biofeedback we thank our numerous colleagues, collaborators, and students.

Preparation of this manuscript and much of the authors' own research reported here were supported in part by grants from the National Heart, Lung, and Blood Institute, HL-14906 and HL-18814 (Dr. Blanchard) and Auburn University Grants in Aid, 74-106 and 75-124 (Dr. Epstein).

Dr. Blanchard is now at the State University of New York at Albany; Dr. Epstein is now at the University of Pittsburgh.

Contents

1

Introduction

Most of you have probably seen the term *Biofeedback*, either in some popular magazine or in an introductory psychology text. It has been hailed by some as the new panacea, able to cure everything from "the heartbreak of psoriasis" to cancer. In fact, there is some evidence, admittedly sketchy, that it can be useful in both of those disorders, as well as in many others.

As indicated by the title, *A Biofeedback Primer*, this is a book designed to give those who are interested in, but have little acquaintance with, biofeedback, an introduction to the field of biofeedback. Thus this book pretends to be neither definitive, comprehensive, nor exhaustive.

Instead, we have sought to give a cursory summary of the two fields of biofeedback: the basic research designed to understand how biofeedback works, and perhaps how the body works; and the applied research designed to test the clinical applicability of this new therapeutic modality.

We have attempted to summarize what is known, point out areas of ignorance, and provide some critical evaluation of the field. Many of the examples cited in detail will be from our own research and clinical experience with biofeedback. We have taken the position of a skeptic: when the data are convincing, we are convinced; but we have remained relatively unimpressed by speculations as to what might be the case. Thus, whether biofeedback is the new panacea is an empirical question, answerable only by sound, empirical data.

A Definition

Having given all of the qualifiers as to what this book is and is not, we would like next to define biofeedback. *Biofeedback is a process in which a person learns to reliably influence physiological responses of two kinds: either responses which are not ordinarily under voluntary control or responses which ordinarily are easily regulated but for which regulation has broken down due to trauma or disease.*

In its more elementary forms, biofeedback consists of at least three operations, most of which are performed electronically. This is depicted in Fig. 1.1.

The first operation is the *detection and amplification* of the biological response. The biological responses can range from the relative occurrence or nonoccurrence of certain brain waves (or electroencephalogram [EEG] rhythms) to levels of activity in certain muscles (or electromyogram [EMG]) to the rate at which the heart

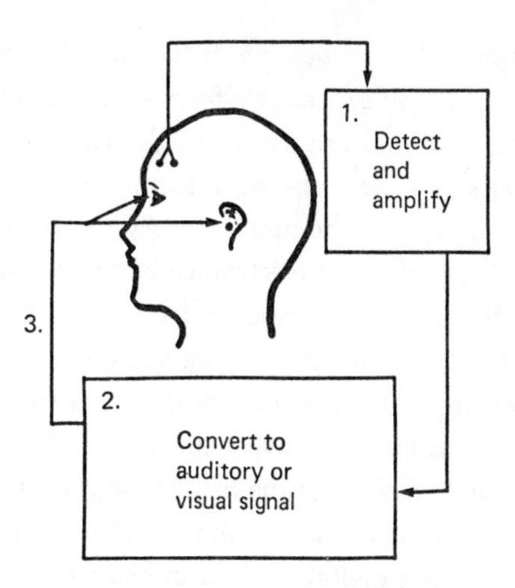

1. Detection and amplification of *bio*electric potentials
2. Convert bioelectric signals to easy-to-process information
3. *Feed* this information *back* to the patient
4. With immediate feedback, patient learns voluntary control response

Figure 1.1

beats. For all of these responses, and the many more to be described later, the naturally occurring slight changes are not detectable by the untrained person but are readily detectable by appropriate measurement devices (transducers) and electronic amplifiers.

For example, most people are not aware of the beating of their heart or the rate at which these beats occur. If it were to stop beating one might become aware of it just before one passed out from lack of oxygen to the brain; if it contracts very strongly and rapidly, as it sometimes does after physical exertion or when one is startled, one is usually aware of it; otherwise the heart continues to beat, relatively unnoticed. As the heart beats, however, it emits a very characteristic electrical signal, the electrocardiogram (ECG), which is fairly easy to measure electronically.

The second operation is the *conversion* of the amplified signal *to an easily* understood or easily *processible* form. We receive most of our information about our environment through visual or auditory modes. Thus we process, or make use of, information in these two modalities better than in any of the other sensory modalities. This second operation is also performed electronically and consists of converting the amplified electronic impulses from the first operation to the appropriate varying auditory or visual signals.

In our heart rate example, the raw electrical signals from the heart, the ECG, are electronically converted, first into a signal proportional to the number of times the heart would beat in one minute if it continued at exactly that rhythm and then is further converted, for example, to a digital readout in beats per minute, the reading of a pen on a meter, or the varying pitch of an auditory signal.

The third operation is the *feeding back to the subject* on a relatively *immediate basis* changes in the signals from the second operation. With this relatively immediate feedback many people can readily gain control of various biological responses, at least while the feedback signal is available.

At this point, it is not clear how long an interval is represented by "relatively immediate." This point will be examined in more detail later in the book. Common practice, however, in both basic research and clinical application is to give the feedback as immediately as possible.

In our heart rate example, common practice is to provide the auditory or visual feedback as immediately as possible, usually within one heartbeat. With such feedback many people can demonstrate some ability to change heart rate voluntarily and a few can show a remarkable degree of control.

Much basic research in biofeedback ends here: either with the demonstration that a particular biological response can be brought under control through biofeedback training or with the discovery or isolation of a particular parameter associated with biofeedback training. In the clinical world, however, that a response can be controlled with the aid of feedback is only a first step. The ultimate clinical goal is either the establishment of self-control, that is, the control of the response in the patient's natural environment in the absence of feedback signal, or a relatively permanent change in the response as a result of the biofeedback training.

A Brief Historical Overview

Biofeedback has a very short history. If one ignores some of the early work in muscle retraining which used feedback of skeletal muscle activity as a way of helping patients to regain control of those muscles but was in no way conceptualized as biofeedback (Maranaci and Horande 1960), then biofeedback is about 15 years old. The term itself did not come into widespread use until 1969.

Four fairly separate lines of research seemed to have converged in the late 1960s to produce the field of biofeedback: studies of operant conditioning of human heart rate and of human galvanic skin response; studies with curarized animals; and studies on the feedback control of the alpha rhythm of the human EEG. A principal impetus to the development of the field of biofeedback was a statement in 1961 by Kimble in his definitive textbook *Conditioning and Learning* (p. 100):

> Thus, for autonomically mediated behavior, the evidence points unequivocally to the conclusion that such responses can be modified by classical, but not instrumental, training methods.

This meant that all of the responses typically thought to be "involuntary" and under the control of or innervated by the autonomic nervous system, such as heart rate, stomach acid secretion, blood pressure, and skin resistance were not subject to instrumental or operant conditioning. Instead, the latter form of learning was thought possible only for responses which were under "voluntary" control such as skeletal muscle responses, etc.

As is typical in psychology, such a clear-cut assertion seems inevitably to prompt other researchers to test it. In so doing, a whole new field of research began. Shortly after the publication of Kimble's (1961) statement, research reports began to appear in which autonomically mediated responses were shown to be modifiable by instrumental conditioning methods. Two of the earliest reports (Shearn 1962; Frazier 1966) each employed a shock-avoidance paradigm in which subjects could avoid mild electrical shocks by making appropriate changes in heart rate. These studies demonstrated that statistically significant increases and decreases in heart rate could both be obtained with these conditions. In fact, Frazier (1966) obtained very large magnitude increases in heart rate. Shortly thereafter, Engel and his associates began a series of studies to show that heart rate could be "operantly conditioned" using a positive reinforcement paradigm rather than shock avoidance.

At about the same time several other researchers, led by Kimmel (Kimmel and Hill 1960; Kimmel 1967, 1974) and later Greene (1966) were showing that galvanic skin response (GSR) could also be operantly conditioned. Interestingly, this line of research seemed to die out eventually while that in other responses has flourished. This could be due to the general lack of clinical utility of the work in GSR biofeedback. (See Chapter 7.) Studies with other autonomically mediated responses followed.

A third line of research which was spawned in part by Kimble's (1961) assertion was that of Miller, DiCara, and their associates with curarized rats. Miller (1969) chose to test Kimble's assertion in animals, more specifically with that mainstay of psychological research, the laboratory rat. One of Miller's goals was to demonstrate unequivocally that autonomically mediated responses could be instrumentally conditioned. To do this, one must be able to rule out clearly any other explanation for the observed results. An early criticism of the work on the operant conditioning of autonomic responses was based on the fact that some voluntarily controlled responses can elicit an "involuntary" or autonomic response. Given that fact, critics argued that what was being conditioned were voluntary responses which elicited the autonomic response rather than directly conditioning the autonomic response itself. (See Chapter 9 for a fuller discussion of mediation issues.)

For instance it is well known that changes in heart rate can be brought about by altering breathing rate and/or depth, or by tensing certain skeletal muscle groups. Both of the latter responses, alteration of respiration patterns and tensing of muscles, are under voluntary control. Thus, if the changes in heart rate, an autonomically mediated response, were "caused" by changes in responses under voluntary control, such a demonstration would not prove that heart rate could be instrumentally conditioned.

Miller hit upon a novel preparation to avoid all question of mediation: laboratory rats were given injections of curare, a drug which paralyzes all skeletal muscles (even those which enable the animals to breathe) by blocking the myoneural synapse. They were then maintained on artificial respiration, which both kept them alive and also regulated their breathing exactly. Finally, as a means of delivering a reinforcement to a paralyzed animal, an electrode was implanted in one of the so-called pleasure or reward centers of the hypothalamus. It has been shown repeatedly (Olds 1958) that mild electrical stimulation of these areas will serve as a reinforcer.

With this preparation, Miller, DiCara, and their associates proceeded to show that not only could heart rate be operantly conditioned, but likewise so could the blood pressure, urine formation, and even the degree of vasoconstriction and dilation in the ear. In one interesting experiment, it was shown that the degree of vasodilation and vasoconstriction in the two ears of the same animal could be conditioned to be different (DiCara and Miller 1968).

This demonstration of large magnitude changes in visceral responses in animals served to encourage biofeedback workers to speculate on a wide range of human psychosomatic disorders which might be treatable with biofeedback. Moreover, this fairly dramatic animal research gave much credibility to the field of human biofeedback during its early days when it sorely needed it. At this time (1969) very little actual clinical application of biofeedback training had been shown. The animal work, however, pointed to a large variety of possible clinical applications.

Unfortunately, after their brilliant series of experiments on operant conditioning of autonomic responses, later attempts at replication did not hold up (Miller and Dworkin 1974). No ready explanation for these later failures has appeared.

Fortunately for the field of human biofeedback, its legitimacy as a field of study and its basic research do not rest ultimately on the animal research. Regardless of the results of future work with curarized animals, human biofeedback research, both basic and applied, has come into its own. There is little direct connection between the animal work and the human work other than that the former may indicate the outer limits for the work with the latter. Clinical biofeedback is not jusified by animal research but rather by its own clinical utility.

The final line of research which led to the field of biofeedback was work in the field of EEG. Several researchers, all relatively independently, began to study whether subjects could "voluntarily" produce certain EEG patterns, particularly the alpha rhythm, a distinctive 8–13 Hz (cycles per second) rhythm. Kamiya (1968) described his work in *Psychology Today* and generated widespread interest. At about the same time, Dr. Barbara Brown was conducting similar studies at the Sepulveda VA Hospital in California. Her initial work focused on the differences in subjective experience subjects reported when their EEGs were different (1970, 1971). In the course of this work she also found some remarkably clever ways to demonstrate feedback control of the brain waves. Finally, Hart (1967) was doing work of a similar nature. Because of the similarity in the subjective experience of a "high alpha state" with that reported for meditation, this work with self-control of the EEG attracted much attention from the nonscientific world and thus helped the whole field to grow.

Fortunately, perhaps, all of these EEG researchers were in California and came to know each other. Dr. Brown became the chief organizer and relayer of information for an informal network of researchers interested in feedback effects on biological responses. This eventually led to the first meeting of this group in Santa Monica, California, in October 1969. From this meeting of some 140 interested persons emerged the term *biofeedback* to describe the whole field and the founding of the Bio-Feedback Research Society.

The Biofeedback Research Society continued to prosper and grow with annual meetings each year and an ever-increasing membership. By 1977 it had over 1000 members and had begun to publish its own journal *Biofeedback and Self-Regulation.* Also in 1976 the name was changed to the Biofeedback Society of America in order to accommodate the growing number of practitioners of clinical biofeedback along with those more interested in research.

Organization of the Remainder of the Book

In the next six chapters the research on biofeedback for five different response systems, cardiovascular, musculoskeletal, electroencephalographic, gastrointestinal, and sexual are considered. The last chapter in this part contains work on several response systems. In each of these chapters, there is a brief description of how the response system works, how it is measured, and how it can be controlled. Next is a summary and integration of the basic research in that response system. Finally, the clinical application research is reviewed.

Chapter 8 contains an analysis and integration of the work on biofeedback, self-control, and self-management from an operant point of view. In the final chapter several current topics are discussed which cut across response systems. The views of other biofeedback authorities are examined and our own speculations on these topics and on the future of biofeedback are included.

2

The Cardiovascular System

Anatomy, Physiology, and Measurement

At the simplest descriptive level, the cardiovascular system consists of the heart, blood vessels, and the blood they contain; it serves primarily to distribute oxygen and nutrients to all parts of the body.

The heart is primarily muscle. It consists of four compartments or chambers. The two upper chambers, called atria (sing., atrium) are both receptacles for returning blood and pumps to force blood into the lower chambers; the two lower chambers, called ventricles, serve as pumps to force the blood through the circulatory system.

Oxygen-depleted blood returns to the right atrium and then is pumped to the right ventricle, the smaller of the two primary pumping chambers. From here it is pumped to the lungs to be reoxygenated. The oxygen-enriched blood returns to the atrium and thence to the major pumping station, the left ventricle. This chamber does most of the heart's work. Its contractions, approximately 72 per minute, force blood out through the arteries to the capillaries and back through the veins. The latter blood vessels, especially the arterioles and the capillary system, offer the major resistance to the flow of the blood.

Four basic parameters define the cardiovascular system in an equation like this:

BP = (CO = HR × SV) × TPR,

where BP is blood pressure;

CO is cardiac output (total blood flow);

HR is heart rate;

SV is stroke volume; and

TPR is total peripheral resistance.

This equation means that blood pressure is directly proportional to the product of cardiac output (which is the product of heart rate and stroke volume, or how much blood is pumped per contraction of the left ventricle) and of total peripheral resistance. The latter refers to the resistance to the flow of blood of the entire circulatory system.

The rate at which the heart beats is normally regulated automatically by two special areas of the heart called the sinoatrial (S-A) node and the atrioventricular (A–V) node. A heartbeat starts at the S–A node, the so-called pacemaker. It then spreads to the A–V node, excitation of which leads to a ventricular contraction.

It is primarily through these two areas that the central nervous system exerts some influence or control over the heart. There are neural connections from both the sympathetic and parasympathetic branches of the autonomic nervous system to both the S–A node and A–V node. Sympathetic nervous system activity leads to increases in the rate of firing of the S–A node, thus increasing HR, and also to sizeable increases in the force of the contraction of the heart muscle, thus increasing stroke volume to some extent. Parasympathetic activity has the effects of decreasing the rate of firing of the S–A node and also slows the rate of conduction of impulses to the ventricles.

The electrical impulses associated with the beating of the heart have, in the normal heart, a very distinct pattern which is recorded as the electrocardiogram (ECG) as shown in Fig. 2.1. One can easily detect each heartbeat by the appearance of this pattern. (Of course, there is an easier way still: by manually monitoring the pulse beat at the wrist in the radial artery or the neck in the carotid artery.)

Ordinarily one does not measure heart rate directly. Instead, one measures the length of time between two heartbeats (interbeat interval or IBI) by counting the elapsed time between two R-waves. Taking the reciprocal of the IBI, we have heart rate. There are electronic devices which accomplish this operation automatically called cardiotachometers. It is also fairly easy to count all of the beats which occur in one minute and automatically record HR in beats per minute (BPM).

Measurement of stroke volume is a very complex task which requires either very invasive procedures such as placing a catheter in-

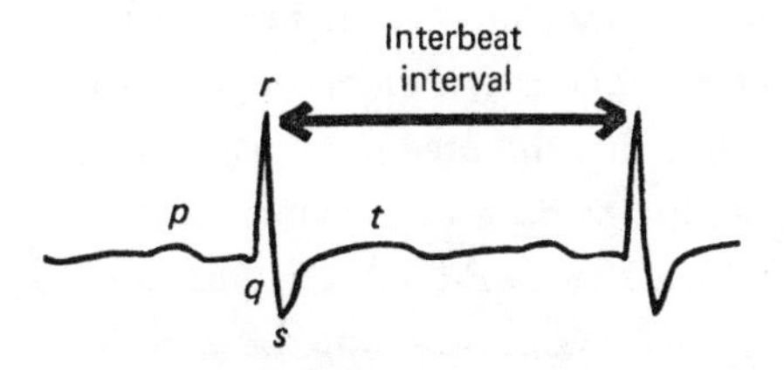

Fig. 2.1 An electrocardiogram.

side the heart or very elaborate measurement and inference. It has not been used in biofeedback work, thus we will not consider it further.

The pressure in the blood vessels is continually varying as the left ventricle contracts, expelling blood, and then relaxes. When you take your pulse manually, you utilize this fact by feeling the mechanical surge of blood "pulsing" through the artery. The pressure in blood vessels varies between two extremes: the maximum pressure is called systolic; the minimum pressure, or resting pressure, is called diastolic. This value is usually expressed in the form of a ratio: systolic BP/diastolic BP, and in units of millimeters of mercury.

The standard way of measuring BP is through ascultation using a device called a sphygnomanometer. A cuff is wrapped around some extremity, usually the upper arm. Attached to the cuff is a pressure-measuring devise. The cuff is inflated until it completely shuts off, or occludes, the flow of blood in the artery. Then the pressure is slowly released while the physician or nurse listens to the artery through a stethoscope. As blood just begins to flow through the artery, a sound, known as a Korotkoff sound, is heard. This pressure is the systolic BP. As the pressure is continually reduced the sounds continue and then fade away. At this latter point, one has determined the resting pressure in the artery, or diastolic BP.

All of these operations can be performed automatically and electronically. However, there is no way, short of inserting a pressure transducer into an artery, to measure BP continuously. It is possible, using a device perfected by Tursky (Tursky, Shapiro, and Schwartz 1972) to obtain a close approximation of BP on a beat-by-beat basis for about a minute. After that the pressure must be reduced to allow the normal circulation to prevent ischemic pain.

There are numerous factors which affect BP (Guyton 1961) and lead to the disease state called hypertension, or elevated blood pressure. One primary cause which has been postulated is increased resistance in the tiny blood vessels called arterioles. To some extent the degree of constriction or dilation (opening) of these vessels is controlled by the sympathetic branch of the autonomic nervous system. Thus increased sympathetic activity could lead to higher BP and conversely, decreased sympathetic activity could lead to reduced BP.

Whereas HR and BP are easily measured and easily quantifiable, there are no good measures of total peripheral resistance. However, it is possible to measure the relative degree of vasomotor tone, the degree of vasoconstriction or vasodilation, at some particular point. The direct measurement is made through photoplethysmography. The latter is a measure of either the amount of light transmitted by the tissue in question, or the amount and wavelength of light reflected by that tissue. Many of you have held a flashlight up to your hand or closed fingers and noticed that some reddish light passes through. This phenomenon is the basis for photoplethysmography. The response recorded is called the vasomotor response and varies with the pulse.

The vasodilation–vasoconstriction response is controlled by the sympathetic nervous system. Depending upon the particular sympathetic fibers activated, the response can be one of constriction or dilation.

An indirect measure of degree of vasoconstriction which has much importance in biofeedback work is surface skin temperature. As the blood vessels, particularly the arterioles, dilate, more blood passes through and the skin surface becomes warmer. Conversely, as the blood vessels constrict, the skin surface cools. Surface temperature is also influenced by the temperature of the room and the body temperature. The latter is usually fairly constant, of course.

Surface temperature is measured readily using a device called a thermistor. This is a material whose electrical properties (resistance) change with changes in temperature. With such a device taped to the finger and connected to the appropriate electronic recording circuit, it is possible to get accurate recordings of changes in skin temperature of 1/10 degree.

The remainder of this chapter is divided into three parts dealing respectively with three different responses: heart rate, blood pressure, and surface skin temperature.

Heart Rate

Judging by the number of published reports on biofeedback and heart rate, one might expect that control of heart rate, and particularly control of heart rate acceleration, was the response of the greatest clinical importance or widest clinical utility. More is probably known about the parameters of biofeedback of heart rate than any other response. By our count over 70 articles have been published in this area. However, when one turns to the clinical application literature, one is hard pressed to find any clinical utility for biofeedback training in heart rate acceleration, with the possible exception that such training is used in one phase of Weiss and Engel's (1971) biofeedback treatment of cardiac arrhythmias, especailly premature ventricular contractions (PVCs).

It is probably the case that heart rate has been much studied for several reasons: it was one of the first responses studied by the biofeedback researchers; it is a response subject to control by both branches of the autonomic nervous system; and, as noted above, it is relatively easy to measure and thus give feedback of. We suspect it is the latter which has led to so much research.

Basic Research

Research on biofeedback with heart rate has had at least three distinct phases: the initial work sought to demonstrate that the phenomena were real and that heart rate could be brought under feedback or operant control. The second phase had two parts: (1) examination of the parameters of the feedback process in an attempt to generate large magnitude changes; and (2) an attempt to understand the vast individual difference one finds in ability to control HR with feedback. The last, and most recent, phase has been concerned with understanding the mechanisms involved, or how they work. Work still continues actively in this area as well as in the area of exploring individual differences.

Phase 1: demonstration of the phenomena

As mentioned above, the first phase of research in biofeedback with HR involved primarily demonstrations that HR could be "operantly" conditioned or changed through the use of biofeedback. This work was dominated by three men, Jasper Brener, Bernard Engel, and Peter Lang, who, with their associates, contributed most of the research in this phase.

The two earliest studies in this phase were those of Shearn (1961) and Frazier (1966). Both studied cardiac acceleration in similar paradigms: subjects (all male) could avoid peripheral electrical shocks by making an appropriate HR response. The experimental situation was designed to deceive the subject, in that he was told he would receive electrical shocks when he was making mistakes on a learning task. In fact, he received electrical shocks either when his HR decreased or when he failed to make continuing increases in HR. In Frazier's (1966) study this was very effective for the four subjects who completed the experiment and led to HR increases of 20 to 60 BPM.

The subjects were never told that HR increases were the response of interest and, according to the reports, the subjects never discovered this. This latter point was probably the beginning of the myth that subjects learned autonomic response control better if they were unaware of what response they were controlling. This myth continued until it was subjected to direct experimental evaluation as will be described later.

Because the work of Engel was both some of the first and some of the most systematic in this field, and because it later served as the bases for his clinical biofeedback work, it will be described in some detail. In the first study Engel and Hansen (1966) sought to operantly condition HR decreases. The small sample of subjects was initially adapted to the experimental situation for a period of 30 minutes. Next came a determination of baseline HR for about five minutes. Finally for the 25-minute experimental trial, subjects were asked to keep both a blinking light on and a running time meter on. The light was controlled by HR: when HR, on a beat-by-beat basis, was less than the baseline level, the light was on; when it went above that level, the light was off. The running time meter accumulated time when HR was below the preset level and stopped when it was above. Subjects were paid one-half a cent per second of accumulated time. Subjects were not told what the response of interest was, only that it was some bodily response, and that their job was to try to keep the light on and the meter running. Control subjects were monitored but the light and clock were controlled by a tape recording of an experimental subject's responses and thus bore no relation to the control subject's behavior.

Results showed that six subjects in the experimental group did decrease their HR significantly below the baseline levels and that as a group they were significantly lower on HR than the control subjects. The average decrease was 0.5 BPM with a range of −2.6 to +2.6 BPM. The control subjects *increased* HR by an average of 5.6 BPM. From the results it appears that the significant difference between groups is due *more* to a sizable average increase on the part of the control subjects than to lowering on the part of the experimental subjects. However, the experimental subjects did lower their HR more than the controls.

The postexperimental interviews revealed a mixture of ideas on the part of subjects as to what response they were trying to control. For the most part the results of these interviews seemed to show that those subjects who were not aware that HR was the targeted response tended to do better whereas those who had some inkling that response was related to HR did poorer. From this postexperimental, or post hoc, data the idea arose that it was better not to inform subjects or that uninformed subjects would show better performance than those who knew what the appropriate response was. This myth persisted for some time until examined directly.

In a second study, Engel and Chism (1967) sought to apply their methodology to operantly condition HR speeding. The arrangements were the same except that the targeted response was increased HR. The results of this study showed that the HR of the experimental subjects was significantly higher than the heart rate for the control subjects. The amount of increase in HR for the experimental subjects averaged 5.9 BPM and ranged from 4.2 to 9.8 BPM. The overall average increase for the control subjects was 3.0 BPM.

In the third study in this series (Levene, Engel, and Pearson 1968) the experimenters sought to determine if subjects could show precise control of HR through being able to alternately raise HR and lower it on successive brief trials within a session. Five subjects were initially given training in speeding and slowing HR similar to that described above for two to four sessions until they met a criterion. They were never informed of the response. There then followed six sessions in which the subject was to alternately increase and decrease HR for one-minute trials throughout an hour-long session. Results showed that two of the five subjects could consistently alter HR significantly while the other three were successful part of the time, usually consistently on either increase ($n=2$) or decrease ($n=1$) trials.

After this study Engel began working exclusively with patients with cardiac arrhythmias, using the same binary visual feedback arrangement. This work is reviewed in a later section of this chapter.

Brener and his colleagues began their work at about the same time as Engel. There are several differences in the methodology of the two investigators: Brener spoke of the effects of "augmented sensory feedback" rather than Engel's "operant conditioning"; Brener tended to report his results in terms of interbeat intervals rather than HR (which makes comparing his work with the work of others somewhat difficult); Brener used binary auditory feedback rather than visual and sought to find differences in HR raising and lowering in the same subjects in the same experiment.

In the first study, Brener and Hothersall (1966) showed that over one session his five subjects clearly learned to discriminate between HR increases and HR decreases with shorter IBIs (higher HR) present 75 percent of the time on increase HR trials and longer IBIs (slower HR) present approximately 70 percent of the time during HR decrease trials. Subjects were not informed and did not guess the correct response.

In the second study, Brener and Hothersall (1967) sought to control respiration rate (RR) and see if subjects could still control HR. After initial training similar to the first experiment, subjects were asked to breathe in time to a paced blinking light, the rate of which was set at their resting RR. Subjects showed they could still show significant discrimination between HR increase and HR decrease trials even with this constraint and could even maintain about a 10 BPM difference.

In the final study of this series, Brener, Kleinman, and Goesling (1969) made a major change in methodology by informing subjects of the response to be controlled. In the first experiment they sought to determine if subjects could control HR without any feedback. Results showed clear-cut discrimination between the ten increase

HR and decrease HR trials in the session with the difference being about 1–3 BPM.

In the second study, feedback was provided for 100 percent, 50 percent, or zero percent of trials while tests of ability to control HR were interspersed. Two such training sessions were held. The results showed that the subjects receiving feedback 100 percent of the time did significantly better than subjects receiving no feedback, both at the first and second sessions. By the second session, subjects receiving feedback on 50 percent of the trials occupied a position between the other two groups. Performance improved from session 1 to session 2 indicating that some learning was occurring.

Taken altogether Brener's work showed (1) that subjects could show significant differences in HR between trials on which they were to increase it and trials on which they were to decrease it, both with, and to a lesser extent, without feedback; and (2) that subjects control HR better with feedback than without it. From this point Brener's work proceeded more into determining the meaning of "voluntary control" and a theoretical model to account for the effects of biofeedback on HR. This will be examined in more detail later.

Lang and his students attacked the problem of demonstrating control over HR in a different fashion: they sought to teach subjects to stabilize HR or to reduce the beat-to-beat variability which occurs naturally in most people. The basic experimental task was the same in all three studies: subjects are presented with a meter on which a pen continually changes relative position on a beat-by-beat basis as the IBI increases or decreases. The subject's task was to try to keep the pen between two lines which represented a range of HR of 4 to 6 BPM. The dependent variables in this type of study are percent time on target, or within the specified range, and a measure of actual HR variability such as the standard deviation.

In the first study (Hnatiow and Lang 1965) experimental subjects received alternating five-minute periods on which they either received or did not receive feedback; the control subjects received false feedback during the "feedback" periods. All subjects were informed of the response to be controlled but the meaning of the actual feedback signal was left vague. Results showed significantly better performance for subjects receiving true feedback over either their own performance without feedback or the performance of control subjects receiving false feedback. Thus it was demonstrated that HR variability could be reduced while absolute HR and RR were unchanged. An attempt by Hnatiow (1971) to replicate these findings failed, probably because of a procedural difference in setting the target range for control. The experimental group ended up splitting almost evenly between very successful and unsuccessful subjects.

In the second major study in this series, Lang, Sroufe, and Hastings (1967) sought to determine the effects both of true feedback and of knowledge of the task on reducing HR variability. Two groups were the same as in the previous study. Two other groups were not told what the feedback display represented but were merely instructed to track the pointer. This condition was controlled for the possible effects of focusing attention on HR variability. Results showed that only the instructed, true-feedback group showed any reduction in HR variability and that reduction was present only when feedback was available. There was again *no* evidence of improvement over successive trials as one might expect in a learning situation.

In the final study Sroufe (1969) sought to replicate the previous findings while introducing a further restriction, control of respiration rate (RR), in a manner similar to that of Brener and Hothersall (1967) with HR control. Some of the subjects learned to breathe at fixed rates determined by a pacing device. Again half of the subjects received true feedback, half false feedback. Results showed that even with RR restricted, subjects could exert a significant degree of control over HR variability. However, subjects given true feedback whose RR was not restricted did better than those for whom RR was restricted, a finding similar to that of Brener and Hothersall (1967). Finally, in this study there was some evidence for learning as subjects receiving true feedback did progressively better over successive feedback trials.

Lang's research on HR variability apparently stopped at this point as he turned his attention to conducting a series of elegant parametric studies of HR biofeedback and also to constructing a theoretical model to account for the HR biofeedback effects.

Comment. The studies just reviewed represent the accumulated knowledge on HR biofeedback at the end of the 1960s. At this point we knew (1) that feedback led to some control of HR increases or decreases and of decreases in HR variability; (2) that binary feedback of either an auditory or visual nature as well as analogue visual feedback helped in controlling HR, but which was best was not known; (3) that true feedback was better than false feedback in controlling HR and grossly better than no feedback; and (4) that subjects could control HR with the use of biofeedback even while simultaneously controlling respiration rate, but performance typically was poorer when RR was also controlled.

Opinion was mixed as to whether subjects should be informed of the nature of the response as was opinion on the utility of contingent rewards. A high degree of individual differences in ability to control HR had been noted. Finally, no one had demonstrated any particularly large scale changes in HR. These issues and others became the concern of the HR biofeedback research of the second phase.

Phase 2: examination of parameters

The research reviewed in this section will be summarized around a series of questions designed to help optimize the biofeedback process.

Is feedback necessary? You will recall that most of the early studies employed control groups which received either false feedback (Engel and Lang) or feedback but no instructions to change

(Lang). Two questions concerning the role of feedback and instructions arose: (1) Is feedback of any variety necessary or sufficient to obtain changes in HR or can changes be obtained through instructions alone? (2) Does the use of feedback add a significant increment to effects obtainable with instructions alone?

Brener *et al.* (1969) demonstrated that subjects could show some difference in HR under the differential instructions to raise or lower HR in the absence of feedback (Study 1) but that subjects obtained significantly more control with feedback than without it (Study 2). However, no directional differences were detectable in Brener's data.

Bergman and Johnson (1971, 1972) provided some additional information on this issue: in the first study (1971) they found that subjects merely instructed to increase or decrease HR showed small (1 to 2 BPM), but significant, changes in HR when compared with an uninstructed control group, over a very brief trial (6 IBIs). In a second study, investigating only HR increases they found instructed subjects could raise HR significantly more (about 2 BPM) than uninstructed subjects and that feedback in the form of hearing heart sounds did not add anything to the effect obtained through instructions alone.

Similar failures to find any advantage for subjects receiving feedback over instructed, no-feedback subjects have been consistently reported by Levenson and his associates (Levenson, 1976; Levenson and Strupp 1972; Manuck, Levenson, Henricksen, and Gryll 1975). In our own work, (Blanchard and Young 1972; Blanchard, Scott, Young, and Edmundson 1974; Young and Blanchard 1974) we have consistently found an advantage in HR increasing for groups receiving feedback over those receiving no feedback but no advantage of feedback in HR lowering. Similar results have been reported by Johns (1970).

A second strategy for comparing feedback to no feedback has involved within-subject comparisons in which subjects are initially instructed to change HR without feedback and later given the same instructions with feedback available. Using such a strategy Lang and Twentyman (1974), Wells (1973), Stephens, Harris, Brady, and Shaffer (1975) and ourselves (Blanchard, Young, Scott, and Haynes 1974) have all found that subjects do much better with feedback than without it in raising HR. Stephens *et al.* (1975) found some advantage for extended feedback training in lowering HR.

When the no-feedback trials follow feedback training, however, frequently there is little or no difference (Bouchard and Corson 1976; Wells 1973; Blanchard *et al.* 1974c) indicating probably that subjects have learned a strategy for HR control which works after feedback is withdrawn.

On the issue of changes in HR obtainable through instructions alone, the evidence supports the notion first advanced by Bergman and Johnson (1971) that subjects can show significant increases in HR through instructions alone (Stephens *et al.* 1975; Wells 1973) despite some failure to find an effect in brief trials (Lang and Twentyman 1974, 1976).

In our laboratory (Blanchard, Young, Haynes, and Scott 1975) we conducted an extended series of trials to determine how much instructional control subjects had over HR acceleration. All sessions consisted of 20 minutes of adaptation followed by 20 minutes of the experimental condition. After a series of four baseline sessions during which subjects rested quietly while attending to their HR, the six experimental subjects were given eight sessions in which they were to increase HR without feedback while the six control subjects continued in the baseline condition. In the final phase, both groups returned to baseline conditions. Results depicted in Fig. 2.2 show a consistent instructional effect with increases averaging 4.8 BPM over the controls and 6.3 BPM over the baseline levels for the experimental subjects.

Comment. Although the evidence is somewhat mixed, we seem to be able to draw the following conclusions on the issues raised in

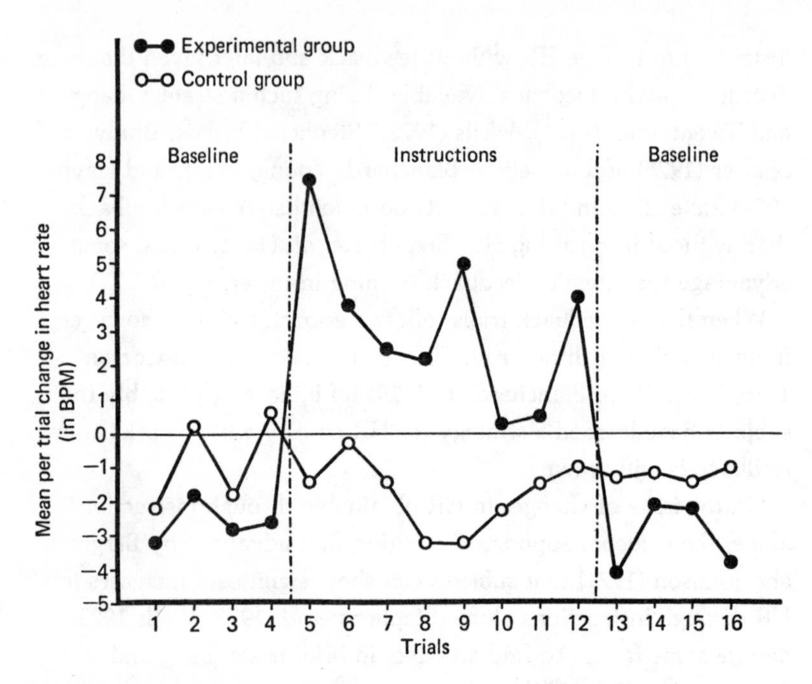

Fig. 2.2. Mean heart rate change for instructed and control groups for each session of the experiment.

this section: (1) subjects can show significant increases in HR when instructed to do so without any prior biofeedback training; there is also limited evidence showing that they can similarly lower HR, but it is much less consistent. (2) When feedback is added to instructions, it usually enables subjects to show significantly greater increases in HR over that obtainable through instructions alone; the evidence for an incremental effect of feedback for HR lowering is completely mixed but probably favors a slight feedback effect.

Which kind of feedback? The feedback signal used as exteroceptive feedback to aid subjects in gaining control of HR can vary in at least two ways: (1) the sensory modality in which the feedback is given (usually auditory or visual) and (2) the amount of information contained in the feedback signal. The two extremes on this dimension are a *binary* signal which informs the subject only of whether he has made the correct response or not and an *analogue* signal which tells him not only whether he is correct or not, but also by how much he has missed or exceeded a target level. The analogue signal thus contains much more information than a binary signal.

You will recall from the previous section that binary feedback in either an auditory (Brener) or visual (Engel) mode helped subjects to learn to control HR and that analogue visual feedback helped subjects reduce HR variability. Shortly thereafter analogue feedback in both the visual (Finley 1970; Sroufe 1971) and auditory (Headrick, Feather, and Wells 1971) modes were added to the growing list of possibilities.

In our laboratory we tried to answer these questions. In the first study (Blanchard and Young 1972) we gave groups of college students analogue feedback (thus holding the information content constant) in both the auditory and visual modalities. A third group received no feedback. Auditory feedback came from a voltage-controlled audio oscillator the pitch of which was proportional to HR. Visual feedback came from a meter's pen which tracked the tachograph signal. All subjects knew that HR was the response to be changed on a series of one-minute trials, some on which HR was to be increased, on an equal number decreased. After the first session, both feedback groups were split and for half the subjects the modality was changed, for half it remained the same. In this way comparisons of the two kinds of feedback could be made both between different groups of subjects and within the same group of subjects.

Results showed that all groups receiving feedback did better than the instructed, no-feedback group in raising HR but were no better at lowering HR. There were *no* consistent differences between the two sensory modalities.

In the second study (Blanchard, Scott, Young, and Haynes 1974), we gave groups of subjects visual feedback in either an analogue or binary fashion. A third group again received no feedback. Again all subjects knew the response to be changed. Subjects initially received four sessions containing both increase HR and decrease HR trials. Then the feedback groups were split and for half the subjects the type of feedback was changed while for the other half it remained the same.

Results clearly favored the analogue feedback for increasing HR: on all comparisons subjects receiving analogue feedback did better than those receiving binary feedback. The performance of the group which initially received analogue feedback and was switched to binary feedback dropped down to the level of the no-feedback subjects. Their counterparts who went from binary to analogue feedback improved performance immediately. For HR lowering there were again no differences between subjects receiving feedback and the no-feedback group.

Lang and Twentyman (1974) obtained similar results for both increasing and decreasing HR in their comparisons between groups given either binary or analogue visual feedback in Lang's (1974) computer-directed biofeedback laboratory. Although they did not make comparisons in groups which received both kinds of feedback, they did extend the findings through no-feedback trials added to the end of the training sessions. In the latter they found that the advantages of analogue feedback held up for HR raising.

Colgan (1977) also replicated these findings in a study which included groups which received either binary, binary plus analogue, or analogue feedback in a visual mode for six acquisition sessions and four extinction sessions. Trials both to increase and to decrease HR were given. Again analogue feedback, either alone or with binary feedback, surpassed binary for HR increases. It also led to significantly greater decreases in HR than binary, a new finding. During the extinction trials the differences held up but in attentuated form.

It would thus appear that analogue feedback with its higher information content is consistently superior to binary feedback. Such is not always the case, however. In another study from our laboratory (Young and Blanchard 1974) five groups of subjects were given different amounts of *auditory* feedback: analogue feedback, binary feedback, a mixture of binary and analogue feedback in which the analogue signal was available only after a criterion level was reached, heart sounds, and no feedback, for two sessions in which subjects were given trials both to increase and decrease HR. Results showed all feedback groups increased HR significantly more than the no-feedback group, but did not differ among themselves. All *five* groups (including the no-feedback group) showed significant lowering of HR, but did not differ among themselves.

Shapiro, Tursky, and Schwartz (1970a) likewise compared binary and analogue auditory feedback in groups of subjects who were to raise or lower HR. Unfortunately they confounded their methodology by providing *all* subjects with binary visual feedback. Results showed significant differences between increase and decrease HR groups, but *no* effects due to feedback modality.

Comment. At this point it appears that the information content of the feedback signal makes a difference (more information leads to better control) when feedback is given in a visual modality but does not make a difference when given aurally. No adequate simultaneous test of all four possibilities has yet been done.

Is reward necessary? Among the pioneer HR biofeedback investigators, Engel and his associates consistently described the biofeedback training process in terms of operant conditioning whereas Brener and his colleagues described it in terms of the effects of information feedback as did Lang. This difference in terminology persists to some extent even today. This distinction is more than a mere matter of semantics, however, for it involves both a basic methodological issue of whether, for best results, subjects should receive some form of tangible reward contingent upon successful performance, and also a conceptual model of how the process works.

Reinforcement, as typically defined by operant conditioners, serves at least two functions: it inherently provides the subject with *information* of a binary nature as to whether his response is correct or not, in that one receives a reinforcement only for successful or criterion level responses; second, it provides an *incentive* for the subject to make appropriate responses. Moreover, since by its functional definition, reinforcement is a contingent stimulus event which leads to a change in behavior, then feedback or knowledge of results about a response will *function* as a reinforcer. In this sense feedback and reinforcement are inextricably confounded for one cannot give feedback which does not function as a reinforcer.

A way out of this dilemma was provided in a study by Blanchard *et al.* (1974c). In a long-term experiment involving 48 sessions, subjects were instructed to increase HR and given binary visual feedback to assist them. Feedback was provided by a running time meter that accumulated seconds during which HR was above a criterion level. The stopping and starting of the clock thus provided the subject with information as to whether HR was above the criterion level or not. After baseline sessions and eight sessions in which the effects of instructions alone were evaluated, subjects received twenty-four 20-minute training sessions on which they were to raise HR. An incentive, or reward, for performance was either added or withdrawn systematically, by making the accumulated time convertible to money. The study was thus a series of replicated single-subject experiments.

Most importantly, care was taken to determine that the payoff rate, approximately ten cents a minute, would *function* as a reinforcer for another task with these subjects. All subjects were given a simple bar press task on which there were alternating five-minute periods of reward and no reward on a FR–30 schedule. The availability of rewards drastically altered the bar press rate thus showing that the reward was a functional reinforcer.

Results of the study showed that all subjects increased HR when feedback was provided, with average increases ranging from 2 to 24 BPM. The addition or withdrawal of reinforcement had no consistent effects: for two subjects there was clear-cut evidence of a reinforcement effect; for one it was present one time but not another, while for the other three reinforcement had no effect.

Lang and his co-workers (Lang 1974; Lang and Twentyman 1976) have provided data showing that monetary incentives do improve performance. In one study a significant effect of monetary incentives versus no incentives was found on HR speeding attempted prior to feedback training and also on HR speeding during feedback trials, with no significant effect on HR slowing. On later transfer trials on which subjects were to continue controlling HR in the absence of feedback, incentives led to significantly better performance on HR slowing but not on HR speeding. The incentive had not been shown operationally to be a reinforcer. Moreover, the effect of incentive seems to vary for no apparent reason. In a second study, Lang (1974) found a pronounced effect of contingent monetary rewards on HR speeding, but not HR slowing, in subjects who had already had four prior training sessions. This seems to indicate a facilitative effect of incentives but lack of proper control procedure leaves this in doubt.

Guenther and McFarland (1973) found no effect of monetary incentive on a task involving fairly precise HR control. In fact, subjects offered the monetary incentive were more variable as a group then those who were not offered incentives. In an additional study, Stephens *et al.* (1975) added a contingent monetary incentive to their combination of binary and analogue feedback for HR increases and decreases after two sessions without it. They found no effect of the contingent incentive on HR lowering or HR raising.

Comment. At this point it is not clear whether contingent rewards for performance in HR control facilitate that performance or not. Certainly in long-term studies the effects are far from universal and in short-term group studies the evidence is contradictory.

As to whether the overall process should be considered as operant conditioning, the answer is also unclear. May and Johnson (1972), in a study involving use of different schedules of feedback for HR lowering in two long-term, single-subject experiments, found that continuous reinforcement (CRF) led to consistent decreases of 4 to 6 BPM, but that performance began to deteriorate as the schedule was thinned to an FR–2 and an FR–3. This would seem to indicate that HR decreases do not respond to schedule effects in the manner of most operants.

Should subjects be informed of the response? In the early days of HR biofeedback training, opinion differed as to whether subjects should be informed of the response to be changed or not; Engel did not inform his subjects, Brener initially did not inform them but later switched (Brener *et al.* 1969) to informing them; Lang showed a similar pattern of changing from not informing to informing subjects. A myth developed, based probably on Engel's reports that subjects who correctly guessed that the response being changed was related to HR performed more poorly than those who did not guess.

In order to determine the effect of knowledge of the response we (Blanchard *et al.* 1974a) performed the following prospective study in which knowledge of the response was treated as an independent variable to be manipulated. Four groups of subjects were given trials at the first session to raise and lower HR: an informed, feedback group, an informed, no-feedback group; an uninformed feedback group, and a misinformed feedback group. At the second session, half of the latter two groups were informed of the correct response while half continued in the original condition.

Results showed that informed subjects did consistently better than all of the other conditions in lowering HR and generally better than the others in raising HR. Only informed subjects consistently showed any evidence of HR control.

Comment. The study above showed conclusively that informing the subject of the correct response was facilitative, and certainly not detrimental. This was of great advantage in clinical work since trying to train patients to control HR for some therapeutic purpose while keeping them uninformed becomes a rather ridiculous, if even unethical, task. Since the early 1970s all studies have informed subjects of the response to be controlled.

Phase 3: individual differences

In their 1973 review, Blanchard and Young listed three studies involving a total of eight subjects for whom large scale (defined as a change of 20 percent of baseline value) HR increases were obtained. Headrick *et al.* (1971) obtained increases in HR of 30 BPM or more in a single subject who was given 12 sessions involving numerous trials. Likewise, Stephens, Harris and Brady (1972) reported on four subjects who obtained increases in HR ranging from 15 to 29 BPM, and decreases of 3 to 6 BPM, over a number of sessions and trials. Each subject was run with a slightly different combination of feedback, reward, and trial length. Finally in our laboratory (Scott *et al.* 1973a), we obtained increases of 16 and 30 BPM in subjects who were run for thirty-four and eighteen 20-minute sessions. We were also able to obtain a 16 BPM decrease in one subject who was run for 52 sessions. From this work it seemed that multiple sessions were necessary to obtain large-scale effects, and that large-scale decreases were practically impossible to obtain.

Since 1973 several other studies have addressed the issue of obtaining large-scale changes in HR. Wells (1973) ran nine subjects in a relatively long training program involving 11 sessions with 20 trials of 90 seconds per session. Half the trials were increase HR, half decrease HR. Results showed that six subjects were able to show large-scale increases in HR, ranging from 16 to 35 BPM; for decreasing HR, the results were poorer: only one subject could decrease HR by at least 3 BPM. Subjects were able by the end of training to maintain the increases in HR in the absence of feedback.

In our laboratory (Scott, Blanchard, Edmundson, and Young 1973b) we were able to demonstrate large-scale increases in HR which could be maintained over at least three consecutive daily trials of 20 minutes each in four subjects: increases ranged from 15 to 40 BPM. In two other subjects stable decreases of 15 BPM were obtained; however, these came in clinical subjects with tachycardia. (See the section entitled Clinical Application.)

Finally, in a major study of large-scale HR control, Stephens *et al.* (1975) presented individual data on 40 subjects who each received five sessions containing four 4-minute HR raising trials and four 8-minute HR lowering trials. Feedback of both an analogue and binary nature as well as contingent rewards were given. Results showed that 19 subjects achieved average HR increases of 10 BPM or greater, and 11 of these had changes of 15 BPM or more, with the top three subjects averaging over 30 BPM. HR decreases, on the other hand, averaged only three BPM: 18 subjects showed average decreases of three BPM or more, while eight of these showed average decreases of five BPM. The best average decrease was 8.7 BPM. It is thus apparent that there are wide individual differences in the ability of a relatively homogeneous population, i.e., college students, to control HR and that HR acceleration is markedly easier in terms of magnitude of response, than is HR deceleration.

Not too surprisingly, the wide range of individual differences in ability to control HR led to attempts to find ways of predicting who could control HR and who could not. As is typical in psychology, the initial way of trying to answer this question was through various self-report measures. Work has focused on three of these: Rotter's (1966) Locus of Control Scale (Internal vs. External Locus of Control); Mandler, Mandler, and Uviller's (1958) Autonomic Perception Questionnaire (APQ); and a measure of manifest anxiety.

The APQ seemed a logical initial candidate since it asked subjects to report how aware, during various situations, they were of various autonomically mediated responses including HR. In the first study, Bergman and Johnson (1971) reported that subjects who fell in the middle third of scores on the APQ showed more ability to control HR acceleration, in the absence of feedback and with only instructions, than subjects who were either more aware or less aware. However, in a later report (Bergman and Johnson 1972), they found no relationship between APQ scores and control of HR.

In our own work Blanchard, Young and McLeod (1972) divided subjects into high and low aware based on the cardiovascular items of the APQ. We found that subjects who reported low awareness of cardiac activity showed significant increases and decreases in HR when assisted by feedback while high awareness subjects showed no control. A replication involving 40 subjects (over three times as many as were involved in the initial study) failed to find any systematic relation between APQ scores and HR control.

This lack of systematic relationship between APQ score and HR control was confirmed in a study by McFarland (1975). At this point it would appear that the Mandler *et al.* APQ is not a good predictor of ability to control HR.

The second line of work involved Rotter's (1966) Locus of Control Scale. This dimension orders individuals from *Internals* who perceive themselves as having a high degree of control over their environment to *Externals* who perceive themselves as having low control of the environment or being more at the mercy of fate. Ray and Lamb (1974) divided subjects on this dimension and gave them brief training in HR control, both increases and decreases in HR, with feedback. They found that the Internals showed significantly better performance in increasing HR while Externals showed significantly better ability to decrease HR. In a later study Ray (1974) replicated this finding. Both groups showed bidirectional control of HR with the assistance of feedback but again Internals were superior in HR increasing and Externals in HR decreasing. Bell and Schwartz (1973) found the same relation for HR lowering but not for raising HR with feedback.

Gatchel (1975) took this research one step further by extending training over two different sessions. At his first HR biofeedback-training session his results replicate those of Ray, Internals are superior at raising HR and Externals are better at lowering. However, by the second session *these differences have completely disappeared!* It thus appears that the I–E trait influences only the initial performance in HR control (a finding replicated by Gatchel [1975] without feedback) but that this difference is wiped out by even one additional training session. Bell and Schwartz (1973) also found that Internals showed better control of HR raising with feedback than Externals.

Stephens *et al.* (1975) found the ability to raise HR and to lower HR were significantly and positively correlated ($r = 0.31$). Also basal HR was related to ability to lower HR but not to ability to raise it. Finally they found that ability to control HR without feedback on trials given at the start of the experiment significantly correlated with ability to control HR raising with feedback ($r = 0.53$). Bell and Schwartz (1975) replicated this result but failed to find any relation between ability to raise HR and ability to lower HR with feedback.

These latter results seem to indicate that subjects enter experiments with some level of ability to control HR. The addition of feedback to instructions enhances this initial ability. For some subjects there is thus little evidence of learning; instead they show their maximum level of performance within the first trial or first few trials. Others, however, gradually acquire control, but indications are that the final level is related to initial ability to control HR.

Phase 4—mechanisms, mediation and theoretical models

One of the first questions asked after a presentation of research results on HR biofeedback training is usually, "How do subjects change their heart rate?" Unfortunately, after ten years of research in this area, there is still no good answer to that question.

One way of answering that question is to ask the people who take part in the experiments. We did this systematically in one study (Blanchard *et al.* 1974) and found some not unexpected results: subjects reported relatively high use (42 percent of total responses) of such things as "thinking of fear or anxiety-arousing things or situations," "thinking angry or aggressive ideas," "thinking of exciting things or feeling excited, aroused, or tense" when raising HR. For lowering HR, 41 percent of the total responses involved "thinking of relaxing things or trying to relax." Bell and Schwartz (1975) reported similar results with over 75 percent of their subjects reporting use of thought categories such as "excitement, sex, fear, tension, and tenseness" for HR raising and "contentment, relaxation, and tranquility" for HR lowering.

In the Blanchard *et al.* (1974a) study, we went a step further and asked, "Do subjects who show good control differ in cognitive strategy from those who show poor control?" We divided the informed subjects who received feedback into two groups based on relative performance in HR raising and in HR lowering and compared their self-reports. *We found that subjects who showed good control and subjects who showed poor control both reported using the same strategies.*

The futility of asking subjects how they control HR during biofeedback training is further highlighted by this incident: a male subject in a study designed to test a particular shaping procedure in HR control (Scott *et al.* 1973b) showed very good HR control with feedback achieving increases of over 160 percent of baseline HR which was maintained over several 20-minute trials. At the end of the study we asked him how he controlled his HR. He told us, in a very frank manner, that he wiggled his left ear. When pressed, he maintained that this was the mechanism he had discovered.

At this point, we tend to agree with Engel (1972) that it is futile to ask subjects how they do it. Each subject seems to have his own idiosyncratic strategy which the subject can test out in the biofeedback situation. For those dissatisfied with this answer, we offer Jasper Brener's solution: Tell someone to raise his arm; then ask him how he did it. The variety of responses to the latter question is similar to what biofeedback subjects give to a query about how they control a response.

A few years ago there was much controversy surrounding the issue of whether instrumental conditioning of autonomic responses could be demonstrated in humans (Katkin and Murray 1968). Part of this argument was that subjects were controlling responses which were known to be "voluntary," such as respiration or muscle tension, and through changing these voluntary responses were changing HR. Several studies followed in which subjects were asked to change HR with the assistance of feedback while respiration was controlled, usually through some sort of pacing procedure (Brener and Hothersall 1967; Johns 1970; Sroufe 1969). The results of these studies were that subjects could still demonstrate control of HR (raising, lowering, or changes in variability) with respiration controlled, but the magnitude of the effects was reduced. Obrist and his colleagues (Obrist 1976; Obrist, Galosy, Lawler, Gaebelein, Howard, and Shanks 1975) have shown convincingly that the fewer constraints one puts on subjects, the better their ability is to change HR. As constraints are added to respiration and skeletal muscle maneuvers, smaller changes are demonstrated; however, even in the most restricted condition subjects could still show significant control of HR. These results taken together seem to mean that subjects ordinarily utilize several mechanisms to assist in controlling HR and that as use of some is prohibited, the magnitude of control diminshes.

Theoretical models[1]. The most recent development in HR biofeedback has been the development of theoretical models to ex-

---

1. We acknowledge the assistance of Don Williamson in preparing this summary of theoretical models of HR control.

plain the results of HR biofeedback studies. Three different prominent biofeedback researchers, Brener, Lang, and Schwartz, following the lead of Engel (1972), have proposed similar, yet different, models of biofeedback effects on the cardiovascular system, based on a motor skills learning approach (Bilodeau and Bilodeau 1969; Fleishman 1966). The latter approach is based on years of research on how human subjects acquire complex motor skills such as riding a bicycle or accurately shooting a basketball.

Brener (1974a) initially provided a useful distinction between voluntary and involuntary responses. Voluntary responses are those which the cooperative subject can show in response to a simple request, such as "Raise your hand."; involuntary or "nonvoluntary" responses are ones which are not under the control of simple instructions.

Brener (1974a, 1974b, 1975) has gone on to propose a general model of voluntary control that is based upon James's (1890) ideomotor theory of voluntary action. In the simplest sense, this model hypothesizes that the development of voluntary control is a function of the degree of "awareness of the response to be controlled" (Brener, 1974a). To avoid the implicit mentalism of the term "awareness," Brener (1974c, p. 585) has suggested that a more appropriate statement would be that his model "proposes that the ability of subjects to discriminate the consequences of their actions is a prerequisite to the development of instructional control over those actions." This model presumes that initial instructions to human subjects activate very undifferentiated, nonspecific response patterns. If the proper response is embedded within this behavioral Gestalt, then the subject receives exteroceptive feedback that he has "done the right thing." Eventually the subject learns to discriminate the interoceptive sensations associated with this "correct response" and learns to initiate it without the aid of exteroceptive feedback. Furthermore, in his article on the development of specificity, Brener

(1974b) has suggested that within certain biological constraints the subject should eventually learn to control specific autonomic functions or response patterns.

Lang (1974, 1975) has focused his attention exclusively upon questions related to the acquisition of HR control. For HR speeding, Lang has suggested that the motor skills learning model is very appropriate. However, for HR slowing, he has produced an abundance of evidence which he interprets as showing that HR slowing should be regarded as pure visceral learning. This distinction between skills learning and visceral learning is important because the two are thought to be controlled by different physiological mechanisms. Lang considers HR speeding to be dependent upon central mechanisms which couple somatic and cardiovascular systems as has been suggested by Obrist *et al.* (1975). On the other hand, he regards HR slowing to be relatively independent of somatic activity and has suggested that it is controlled by the learned modification of vagal tone (Lang and Twentyman 1974).

In support of Lang's model, numerous studies (e.g., Blanchard *et al.* 1974b; Lang and Twentyman 1974) have reported differential findings for the tasks of heart rate speeding and slowing. Also, Gatchel (1974) has reported that the frequency of feedback affected the performance of subjects for HR speeding, but not for slowing. Furthermore, several studies have reported that subjects could immediately produce large magnitude HR increases, but not decreases.

Schwartz (1974, 1975) has also adopted the motor skills learning approach, but his interests have mainly concerned the effects of feedback upon the learned control of response patterns. He has suggested that the specific response pattern that is learned via biofeedback training is a function of two factors: (1) the specific feedback contingency and (2) biological constraints. Thus Schwartz has hypothesized that if subjects are given feedback information of a specific response pattern, e.g., raise HR and lower systolic BP, the subject will learn to control this specific response pattern unless there are certain biological constraints which mitigate against such learned control. Like Brener, Schwartz (1975) has hypothesized that under these conditions, response specificity emerges from a more generalized physiological arousal.

Clinical Applications

Even though much is known about biofeedback effects on HR, there are few disorders in which HR, per se, is the clinical problem. Instead, for most of the applied research, patients have been trained to control HR in order to obtain a therapeutic effect on some other clinical problem.

Cardiac arrhythmias

As described in the first part of this chapter the normal operation of the heart involves rhythmic, synchronized contractions which begin at the S–A node. From time to time because of various defects and cardiovascular diseases, this normal rhythmic operation, known as the "sinus rhythm," is interrupted either regularly or episodically. When this occurs, the patient is said to have a *cardiac arrhythmia.* Some of these arrhythmias are very serious and if uncontrolled could lead to death fairly quickly. Others are less serious but still warrant treatment.

The first published reports of the use of HR biofeedback with clinical problems were those of Engel and his associates. After several preliminary reports (Engel and Melmon 1968; Weiss and Engel 1970), Weiss and Engel (1971) published data on a series of eight patients with premature ventricular contractions (PVCs). This study will be described in some detail because it is one of the most frequently cited clinical applications of biofeedback.

As implied in the term, premature ventricular contractions represent early, or premature, contractions of the ventricles rather than these contractions following the atrial contractions with the appropriate lag. As a result, the ventricles are incompletely filled with blood and overall cardiac output decreases. This problem is the result of some local area of the heart muscle acting as a "pacemaker," or source of initiation of beats, rather than the S–A and A–V nodes.

Although the number of Weiss and Engel's patients who completed the various phases of the HR training program varied, a more or less standard training program was used with phases of approximately ten sessions each. The training in HR control closely replicated the early basic research of Engel: patients were taught to increase HR, then to decrease HR, and then alternately to increase and decrease HR for one- to three-minute periods. Next the patient was taught to reduce the variability of his HR (similar to Lang's [1967] early work) by holding it within a specified range. An important feature of this phase was that the feedback apparatus, approximately the same binary visual feedback arrangement used in Engel's research with normals, gave patients direct feedback of the occurrence of a PVC.

In the last phase, self-control training was begun. While the patient was keeping his HR within the specified range, feedback was systematically faded out: first one minute on and one minute off; then one on and three off and finally one on and seven off. In this manner patients learned to control both HR variability and the occurrence of PVCs without the aid of feedback, thus moving from feedback-assisted control to true self-control.

All training was done while the patients were hospitalized and consisted of one to three sessions per day with approximately 34 minutes of training per session. Patients also had their ECGs monitored while they were in bed at the hospital.

Three of the eight patients completed the entire training program; one more completed all but the final part of the fading out of feedback during range training and another completed the first part of the feedback fade-out training. Of the other three patients, two had training in increasing and decreasing HR and holding it within the specified range while the final patient had training in HR slowing and holding it within the specified range.

Much to their credit the authors obtained follow-up data on all eight cases. In four patients there was a marked decrease in rate of PVCs. For these four patients, the pretreatment rate was 10-20 PVCs/minute; at the end of treatment and at follow-up (up to 21 months after the completion of training) the rate was about one PVC/minute. These four patients can all be considered clear-cut successes. In a fifth patient there was a noticeable decrease in PVC rate. For the other three patients, there was no evidence of reduction in rate of PVCs.

A valuable feature of this article was the systematic presentation of data on the dependent variable of most interest, the rate of emission of PVCs, as well as on HR itself. From these data we can determine how well patients actually learned to control their HR and in which training phase the major improvement, that is, reduction, in PVCs occurred. For two patients the major reduction in PVCs occurred during alternation training; for two other patients the reduction occurred during *range* training; however, one patient who eventually improved did poorer during range training. For the final patient who showed improvement, there was a reduction in PVC rate during training in HR slowing and a further reduction during alternation training. Thus, there does not seem to be a consistent relationship between training phase and decrease in PVC rate.

An interesting relationship emerges, however, if one reexamines the results of this study from the point of view of length of treatment. Those patients who received more treatment, that is, more training sessions, tended to improve whereas those who received less treatment did not. If one divides the patients into those receiving 47 or more training sessions and those receiving less than 47 sessions, then by Fisher's Exact Probability Test, there is a significant ($p < 0.05$) relation between treatment outcome and treatment length.

In three patients separate pharmacological studies were done in an attempt to isolate the neurological mechanisms responsible for the changes. This work suggested that a decrease in sympathetic nervous system activity was responsible for decreased PVCs in one case and that an increase in parasympathetic (vagal) activity was responsible in a second case.

Regardless of the mechanisms involved, this was a very influential study. Unfortunately, because of some flaws in experimental design, it is not possible to rule out expectancy or placebo effects as being responsible for the results. Moreover, the relationship between improvement and training phase are bothersome.

In a more recent report (Engel and Bleecker 1974) Engel has replicated his earlier findings in another single patient with PVCs. Baseline recordings of PVC rate were obtained for the first time and found to be approximately 15 PVC/min. The patient was then put through a training program similar to the earlier one: training in HR slowing, HR speeding, and alternate slowing and speeding. The final phase was training in holding HR within a specified range. Rate of PVCs dropped during the HR slowing to about 5 PVC/min; there was further decrease to almost zero during HR alternation training. At follow-up, the patient had no PVCs.

In any type of research, replication is important. In clinical research, especially in an area such as biofeedback in which the possibility of placebo effects seems greater than usual, replication by an independent investigator is very important. Pickering and Gorham (1975) reported on the biofeedback treatment of a woman who had PVCs, the frequency of which seemed related to basal HR. As her heart speeded up, during normal exercise, she began to emit PVCs, especially above an HR of about 78 BPM.

Training consisted of 16 sessions over six weeks and was primarily in alternation of HR: one minute speeding, one minute slowing, one minute rest. She gradually learned to increase her HR by as much as 25 BPM, but never showed much ability to lower her HR. This ability transferred to trials on which feedback was withheld. As a result of the training the basal HR at which the PVCs began shifted upwards to about 94 BPM; furthermore, when the PVCs began she could lower her HR to a level at which they were greatly diminished.

In our own laboratory we ran a 66-year-old woman with PVCs through a training program of 47 sessions spread over a four-month period, using many of the same conditions as described by Weiss and Engel (1971). The patient was seen as an outpatient and never more than three times per week. During the baseline phase she was emitting approximately 10 PVC/min. The results of training were highly variable and the patient never demonstrated any consistent ability to suppress PVCs. Her best results came during a set of three consecutive sessions during alternation training: she reduced her PVC rate from 12 PVC/min to about 3 PVC/min within the session and maintained it during a no-feedback, self-control portion. However, this ability did not hold up during later sessions.

A second cardiac arrhythmia for which there have been several reports of biofeedback treatment is *sinus tachycardia.* In this arrhythmia, the heart beats with the normal sinus rhythm but at an abnormally high rate. Since in this disorder the clinical response of interest is also the response for which feedback is given, treatment in this instance is aimed at direct modification of an abnormal physiological response.

Engel and Bleecker (1974) treated a woman with a four-year documented history of chronic sinus tachycardia. Although by history her resting HR was 106 BPM, during the initial phase of treatment it was only 86 BPM. Treatment consisted of 12 sessions in which she received binary visual feedback of HR and instructions to lower it. In the next nine-session phase, feedback was gradually faded out in the same manner described for the patients with PVCs treated by Weiss and Engel. By the end of treatment the woman's HR was measured as 68 BPM in the laboratory and 75 BPM as measured independently by her personal physician.

Although clinically this case was a success, since the lowered HR generalized outside of the laboratory, experimentally one cannot be sure what part was played by the biofeedback treatment. The experimental design used does not permit us to rule out a simple habituation process. The in-session data, however, did seem to indicate that the patient gradually acquired some ability to lower HR.

Work from our laboratory with outpatients (Scott *et al.* 1973b) provides independent confirmation of the value of HR biofeedback training in the treatment of chronic sinus tachycardia. Using single subject experimental designs, Scott *et al.* were able to isolate the biofeedback treatment as being responsible for the change.

In the first case a 46-year-old male with a 20-year history of tachycardia was given these conditions: three baseline sessions, during which he rested quietly and watched television; 26 sessions with one kind of feedback arrangement which led to essentially no change, but provided a good control for attention and placebo effects; 18 sessions with an improved binary feedback procedure which led to a reduction in HR to the normal range. A return to baseline conditions for six sessions led to a partial reversal but HR stabilized at 77 BPM.

Concomitant with the improvement in HR were other clinical improvements: the patient actively sought and obtained employment after being on disability compensation for his tachycardia; he decreased his use of minor tranquilizers and also reported that he felt less anxious. An 18-month follow-up revealed that the patient was still employed.

In the second case HR was reduced from a baseline average of 96 BPM to 78 BPM after 19 training sessions. During the return to baseline, no increase in HR was noted; while this is the desirable clinical effect, experimentally the lack of reversal leaves one in doubt as to the role of biofeedback in the change. There was some concomitant clinical improvement in this patient also: he reported feeling less anxious and being able to do more chores at home, but he did not return to work.

Engel and Bleecker (1974) also reported on the treatment of several other arrhythmias including supraventricular tachycardia and paroxysmal atrial tachycardia with some clinical success. However, the reports were too limited and the experimental designs such that the results remain only suggestive.

Comment. At this point the work on the use of HR biofeedback for the treatment of cardiac arrhythmias is in need of more controlled clinical research. Certainly the pioneering work of Engel and his associates in treating PVCs, which has been partially replicated by Pickering, seems to indicate that this arrhythmia is treatable by biofeedback. The same can be said for chronic sinus tachycardia. Beyond this, however, definite conclusions cannot be drawn at the present state of our knowledge.

Nontherapeutic applications of heart rate biofeedback to patients

In addition to the studies in which HR biofeedback has been used for therapeutic purposes, there have been several studies in which patients with some form of cardiac disease have been given HR-biofeedback training, for the purpose of obtaining a better understanding of cardiac mechanisms. The basic notion in all of these studies is that HR can be treated as an independent variable, to be manipulated behaviorally through biofeedback training, rather than pharmacologically.

There is a cardiac disorder called a *complete* (or third degree) *heart block* in which the conduction pathways to the ventricles from the normal cardiac pacemaker, the S–A node, are completely cut off and ventricular contractions come under the control of a separate, slower, pacemaker. Weiss and Engel (1975) sought to determine if a patient with such a disorder could learn, with the aid of feedback, to control the ventricles alone. In the three patients they ran, none could consistently increase ventricular rate (VR) which seems to indicate that the conduction path between the atrial and ventricles must be intact in order for biofeedback to affect VR.

In another study Bleecker and Engel (1973a) trained six patients with atrial fibrillation to control ventricular rate. All six patients showed some degree of control of VR after the biofeedback training which seems to indicate that the control is mediated by neural connections to the A-V node.

In a third study by Bleecker and Engel (1973b), a patient with a cardiac conduction disorder, the Wolff-Parkinson-White syndrome (WPW), was taught to control her HR through a series of biofeedback training sessions similar to those used by Weiss and Engel. Eventually, through an elaborate ECG monitoring and feedback arrangement, the patient was able to learn to control the conduction pattern in her heart, alternating between normal conduction and WPW conduction. Although the patient demonstrated good control in the laboratory, even when feedback had been faded out, there was no long-term therapeutic effect.

In a final study of this category, Lang, Troyer, Twentyman, and Gatchel (1975) studied the relative abilities of three groups of males: healthy college students, middle-aged patients with ischemic heart disease who were ambulatory, and age-matched controls for the latter group who were healthy, to raise and lower HR with the assistance of feedback. In general, they found superior performance by the college-age males in both increasing and decreasing HR with feedback, followed by the healthy middle-aged subjects, and finally the patients. Most of the differences were trends ($p<0.10$) but were clearly consistent. The patients never showed any significant degree of control of HR, either speeding or slowing.

Comment. This nontherapeutic biofeedback work with patients seems to be a fruitful means to study cardiac mechanisms and has been used to great advantage by Engel and his co-workers. Certainly this strategy seems equally as valuable as changing cardiovascular parameters through drugs, since the effects are readily reversible.

Heart rate control and fear responses

It has long been known that subjects' reports of fear or anxiety are frequently accompanied by increases in HR or HR variability, due probably to the increased sympathetic nervous system activity which accompanies the "fight-or-flight" response (Lang 1969; Leitenberg, Agras, Butz, and Wincze 1971; Prigatano and Johnson 1974). Moreover, in our laboratory (Scott *et al.* 1973b) and in the reports of other investigators such as Headrick *et al.* (1971), it has been noted that some "normal" subjects, who achieve fairly high levels of cardiac rate acceleration with biofeedback training, also report feelings of tension and anxiety during the session. These observations lead one to see that the self-report of "fear" or "anxiety" and the physiological response of HR acceleration covary, at least in some individuals.

Some investigators have sought to extrapolate from these findings in this way: if a high HR is associated with reports of being fearful and anxious, would a lowered HR lead to the opposite feelings? Thus, if anxious patients with an increased HR could be taught to lower their HR through biofeedback training, they might become less anxious which would mean that they would make different self-reports (being less fearful) and would decrease their avoidance behavior. Such work would represent direct intervention with one aspect of the physiological response found in fear and anxiety.

Two analogue studies have been conducted to test this reasoning. In the first (Sirota, Schwartz, and Shapiro 1974) two groups of normal female subjects were trained with HR feedback, rewards for appropriate HR responses, and instructions either to increase or to decrease HR during a series of 15 second trials. Half of the trials were followed by two-second peripheral electrical shocks in a range previously reported by each subject to be from uncomfortable to painful. Subjects were asked to rate the painfulness of each shock after it occurred.

The degree of HR control shown by the subjects, as shown by differences between the HR increase group and HR decrease group at the end of training was statistically significant ($p<0.001$) and of reasonable magnitude, 11 BPM. However, the manner in which it took place is somewhat unusual. The HR increase group showed no increase in HR; instead they finished the experiment at the same level of HR as they began. The HR decrease group showed a large scale decrease in HR, approximately 11 BPM. Recalling the data from a previous portion of this chapter, one can see that this is better results on a group basis than anyone else has ever reported.

A possible explanation for this large-scale decrease may be in the timing of the experiment. Subjects were only adapted for five minutes; the remainder of the experiment took about 36 minutes. It seems quite possible that the large-scale decrease was a result of habituation of HR rather than any "learning." In our own work we have found it typically takes at least 20 minutes to achieve 90 to 95 percent of habituation.

Regardless of whether feedback control of HR was shown or not, the subjects with the lowered HR did show a trend toward rating the shocks as less painful than did the subjects whose HR remained at initial levels. This nonsignificant trend, although interesting, does not seem to warrant the authors' claim that teaching subjects HR control could "serve as a behavioral strategy for changing anxiety and fear reactions" (Sirota *et al.* 1974, p. 261).

The second analogue study (Prigatano and Johnson 1972) involved spider-fearful college students. The level of fear of these students was assessed by both self-report and behavioral avoidance (motoric) tests. Half the subjects then received two hours of HR-biofeedback training to keep HR relatively stable while the other half of the subjects had a comparable focused attention control procedure.

Results of the posttreatment assessment revealed similar decreases in fear of spiders by both groups on both self-report and behavioral measures. Moreover, the biofeedback-trained subjects showed no greater control of HR variability than the untrained subjects. This experiment thus fails to provide any support for the idea that learning to control HR would lead to reduction in fear.

A related study by Nunes and Marks (1975) tested the hypothesis with a clinically phobic population. During the treatment of phobias through prolonged in vivo exposure to the feared object, feedback of HR was alternately present and absent for 30-minute periods. Patients were asked to lower their HR with the aid of the feedback.

Results showed that the patients did lower HR slightly, but significantly (3.0 BPM $p < 0.02$), when feedback was available. However, reports of subjective anxiety did not change as a result of feedback, nor did the ultimate course of treatment. Thus, while the biofeedback training in this report was successful, unlike that in the Prigatano and Johnson study, it did not increase the efficacy of the treatment, like the Prigatano and Johnson results.

A recent case report from our laboratory (Blanchard and Abel 1976) demonstrates the use of biofeedback training to counteract the cardiac acceleration which often accompanies anxiety. The patient was a 30-year-old-female with a 16-year history of "fainting spells." She had had numerous medical workups for her condition, technically called a psychophysiological cardiovascular disorder. Thoughts related to the rape she had experienced at age 14 triggered episodic tachycardia.

In order to elicit the problem behavior in the laboratory, audiotapes were developed which captured the ideation that triggered the spells. This was confirmed during baseline sessions in which the patient showed a consistent cardiac acceleration, reaching levels of over 140 BPM and much report of anxiety and distress. After the four baseline sessions, the patient was taught over eight sessions to lower her HR while listening to neutral audiotape. Next she received 25 sessions in which she practiced lowering her HR with the help of the biofeedback while listening to the rape description. Finally, she was returned to listening to the rape description with no feedback to assist her (baseline conditions).

The patient readily learned to lower her HR and gradually became able to lower it while listening to the rape description. This ability persisted when feedback was withdrawn and during follow-up. Moreover, her "spells" disappeared, she became able to engage in many previously avoided behaviors, and was in general less anxious. These gains persisted at a six-month follow-up.

We have recently replicated these results in a young man with multiple phobias which centered around his fear of having a heart attack and dying. He was also taught to control his HR while listening to audio descriptions which captured the ideation of his phobia. Over the course of treatment he showed the ability to reduce HR in the face of this previously arousing situation. Moreover, he reports being less anxious and being able to engage in formerly avoided activities.

A final example of this clinical use of HR biofeedback is provided in a case described by Wickramasekera (1974). This patient had over five years become debililated as a result of recurrent panic attacks and fears that he was having a heart attack. He had over 25 visits to the Emergency Room because of these attacks. He was taught to control his HR through biofeedback training. As a result of fairly brief training (16 sessions), he ceased having panic attacks and was able to return to a normal level of functioning.

Comment. Although the data are somewhat limited, these last three cases seem to illustrate that HR-biofeedback training can be useful in the treatment of certain fears and phobias. The key elements to successful application seem to be (1) that the patient shows a clear-cut HR acceleration to the anxiety-provoking situation and (2) that much of the fear can be related to cardiac function and perhaps fear of eventual heart attack. Given these two conditions, a direct intervention with the physiological response seems warranted. However, much more research is needed in this area to confirm this idea.

Blood Pressure

Research in the control of blood pressure through biofeedback has followed a course of development similar to that with HR: the initial research was with subjects with normal BP (called *normotensive)* while more recent research has focused largely on clinical application. In fact, the bulk of the biofeedback research with BP has centered on teaching patients with elevated BP (called *hypertensive)* to lower their BP. This is not too surprising given the magnitude of the health problem represented by hypertension. (It is estimated that from 10 to 20 percent of the adult population of the United States suffers from elevated blood pressure.)

Basic Research

Harvard group—phase 1

Basic research in the control of BP through biofeedback has been dominated by a research team from Harvard University: David Shapiro, Bernard Tursky, and Gary E. Schwartz. Recall from our earlier description that, unlike HR which is relatively easy to monitor continuously, BP is very difficult to monitor on a continuous basis. BP varies moment by moment between two values, the highest or systolic pressure, and the lowest or diastolic pressure. Moreover, these two extreme values also tend to vary over time and situation. The only way to measure BP directly would be to insert a small tube, called a cannula, into an artery and connect it to a pressure-measuring device. Since this procedure is fairly uncomfortable and somewhat dangerous, it is impractical both as a research methodology and for long-term treatment. This technical problem of how to measure BP and give feedback of it on a continuous basis was solved by the Harvard group as described below.

If one inflates a cuff on a subject's arm to a pressure just above the systolic BP, no Korotkoff sounds are detected in the artery distally (away from) of the cuff, but the pulse can still be detected proximally (nearer to) of the cuff. In the unoccluded arm, however, the pulse would be detected distally almost immediately (within a few milliseconds) after it was detected at the proximal monitoring site. If one varies the pressure in the cuff gradually until one is detecting the joint occurrence of the two signals about 50 percent of the time, the cuff pressure now represents the systolic BP. The Harvard group devised a control system which would keep the pressure in the cuff automatically at the systolic BP or distolic BP, even as this pressure itself varied. It was a relatively easy matter to add a system to feed this information back to the subject in some usable form. Thus was born their "automated constant cuff-pressure system."

The feedback system would work like this: if, for example, the desired response was a decrease in systolic BP, feedback would be given the subject if no Korotkoff sound was detected following the occurrence of a pulse beat (or possibly the R wave of the ECG) within a specified interval. Had a Korotkoff sound been detected, indicating that the subject's systolic BP was above the pressure in the cuff, then no feedback would be given. As the subject was repeatedly successful (no Korotkoff sounds), the pressure in the cuff would be gradually lowered so as to challenge the subject constantly. (For a more complete technical description of the system, see Tursky, Shapiro, and Schwartz 1972. This feedback system is available commercially from Lexington Instrument Co., Waltham, Mass.)

In all of their BP biofeedback studies, Shapiro and his colleagues used the same basic experimental procedure: on each heartbeat, a subject received binary feedback, both visual and auditory, as to whether his BP is just at, or in the appropriate direction away from, a criterion pressure; in addition to the sensory feedback, the subject received a reward of a brief presentation of a slide of either a nude, a landscape, or an indication of a small financial reward on some fixed-ratio schedule for appropriate BP responses. Typically subjects were given 25 trials per session with a trial lasting 50 heartbeats (or usually less than 45 seconds). Between trials the cuff was completely deflated so that natural circulation was restored and the buildup of ischemic pain was prevented.

The Harvard group's initial studies were designed to demonstrate that biofeedback training could lead to changes in BP. In the first study (Shapiro, Tursky, Gershon, and Stern 1969) one group of normotensive male college students was given feedback and rewards to increase systolic BP while another group was to lower BP. Neither group was informed of the response. At the end of the session the average BP of the two groups was significantly different with the decrease-BP group approximately four millimeters of mercury (4 mm Hg) lower than the increase group.

The second study (Shapiro, Tursky, and Schwartz 1970b) was a replication of the first to which a control group receiving random feedback was added. Again the increase-BP and decrease-BP groups were significantly different on systolic BP from each other with the decrease group approximately 3.5 mm Hg lower than the increase group. Interestingly, neither the increase-BP nor the decrease-BP group was different from the random feedback group. At a second session, ten minutes after the first, all subjects were taught to lower BP. In-session baseline BPs for all groups, *prior* to biofeedback training, were all significantly lower than at the end of the first session, despite the fact that the subjects had been disconnected from the equipment and forced to walk around. Only the random group showed a significant decrease in BP within the second session.

The third study (Shapiro, Schwartz, and Tursky 1972) sought to extend the results: similar procedures were followed except that diastolic BP was the response to be controlled and slightly longer training was given. By the end of biofeedback training, the increase and decrease groups were again significantly different. The increase-BP group had raised BP by an average of 4 mm Hg and the decrease group had lowered BP by an average of about 3 mm Hg. In the extinction sessions, during which feedback and reward were withheld, those subjects who were asked to continue controlling BP did so; in fact, the increase-BP subgroup showed a further increase to about 8–9 mm Hg above initial baseline.

Comment. While this series of studies was an impressive pioneering effort, they present some problems also. First, the magnitude of change is small, averaging about 1–2 mm Hg for increases and 4–6 mm Hg for decreases. In some instances the increase-BP groups do not remain above baseline levels (Shapiro *et al.* 1969). Part of the reason for this finding may be the relatively short adaptation and baseline periods used by these investigators, usually five minutes. In our experience at least 20 minutes are needed to adapt a subject to 90 percent of true baseline level. It may be that the lowering of BP found in these studies is primarily an adaptational effect.

Second, none of the studies included an instructed, no-feedback control group to assess the efficacy of this procedure over merely instructing subjects to change their BP. In the one study in which a random feedback control group was included, (Shapiro *et al.* 1970b) neither of the experimental groups showed final BPs significantly different from it.

Finally, it is not possible to tell what are the active ingredients in the Harvard group's procedure since subjects receive both binary auditory and visual feedback as well as rewards on a fixed-ratio schedule. Whether the rewards (termed reinforcers, but see earlier comments on this issue, p. 29) play any part is not known.

Similar questions arose in the HR-biofeedback work and later research provided answers. Recent research by a team (Fey and Lindholm 1975) not connected to the Harvard group, but using a BP-feedback system similar to theirs, has served this function. In their study Fey and Lindholm (1975) gave subjects only binary visual feedback (no rewards) and ran them for three consecutive daily sessions. Four groups were run: decrease-BP, increase-BP, random feedback, and no feedback; the first three were told that BP was the response but not the direction of change, the no-feedback group, unfortunately, was not told what the response of interest was.

Results showed that the decrease-BP lowered BP significantly in each session, and also improved across sessions, reaching a level 9 mm Hg below baseline in the third session. The other three groups did not differ. Thus this study cleared up several issues but still left unresolved the question of how well instructed subjects who receive no feedback could do. It also replicated the failure of the increase-BP group to raise BP above levels obtained through random feedback.

Harvard group—phase 2

Instead of seeking to clarify some of the issues raised by their initial research, the Harvard group's research went in a new direction: to study the effects of biofeedback training on the patterning of cardiovascular responses, especially the degree of integration and differentiation. Recalling the defining equation at the start of this chapter, one would expect that BP and HR would tend to covary, that is, as one increases the other would be expected to increase. This is what is meant by integration; differentiation means that the two responses move in opposite directions.

In the first study of this series (Shapiro *et al.* 1970a), subjects were given feedback and reinforcement for increasing or decreasing

HR while BP was also monitored. Although the HRs of the two groups were significantly different by the end of training by about 6 BPM, BP was not. Reanalysis of data from a previous study (Shapiro *et al.* 1969) showed that, when BP was the response to be changed, it was different in the different conditions but HR was not. (The authors achieved these results in a somewhat unusual way by selecting the subjects in each group who showed the most change on the targeted response, rather than comparing all the members of each group.)

In the second study (Schwartz, Shapiro, and Tursky 1971), integration was demonstrated through an arrangement which gave feedback and reward when HR and BP both changed in the desired direction. A high degree of integration was demonstrated with BP differences of 7 mm Hg and HR differences of 7 BPM between the increase and decrease groups.

In the final study (Schwartz 1972a) attempts were made to condition both integration and differentiation. Again looking at the defining equation, one can see that it should be difficult to have a subject increase BP while decreasing HR or vice versa. However, Schwartz was able to achieve this to a statistically significant degree.

This research showed that at least to a limited extent, HR and BP could be decoupled through the use of the appropriate feedback arrangement. However, it also showed that integration, or joint covariation, was easier to obtain and could lead to sizeable changes in normotensives.

Other basic research in blood pressure

At about the same time that the initial results of the work by the Harvard group were appearing, another biofeedback researcher, Jasper Brener, was developing a system for giving feedback of BP. The system is similar to that of the Harvard group in that the pressure in an occluding cuff varies and is automatically adjusted to hold it near the systolic pressure. The system has two major differences, however: (1) pressure is taken from the last joint of the left index finger, thus obviating the problem of venous return and ischemic pain, and (2) feedback was directly proportional to cuff pressure rather than of a binary nature.

In the one study conducted with this biofeedback system (Brener and Kleinman 1970) two groups of normotensives were compared: one received feedback and instructions to lower BP while the other received feedback but no instructions. The instructed group lowered systolic BP by approximately 16 mm Hg while the control group was unchanged. In the second session, the experimental group lowered BP by about 10 mm Hg, to approximately the same final BP level as in session 1, while the controls were unchanged. HR decreased gradually (6–10 BPM) across trials within a session for both groups but was not related to differential BP effects.

Comment. These results are certainly more impressive than those of the Harvard group with similar subjects trained for comparable periods of time. The greater changes found by Brener and Kleinman, (1970) could be due to the use of analogue feedback (which was shown in HR biofeedback studies to be more effective than binary feedback) or could be due to the measuring site. Our guess is the latter, especially in light of the work in the last section of this chapter which shows that the degree of vasodilation in the hands can be controlled greatly with feedback. It is probably easier to lower the BP through changing vascular resistance in one fingertip than in the whole arm.

Miller and his colleagues (Miller, DiCara, Solomon, Weiss, and Dworkin 1970) also developed a device for continuously monitoring and giving feedback of diastolic BP. However, except for a notable clinical case to be described later, no systematic research using it has been reported. Finally, Elder and his students (Welsh, Elder, Longacre, and McAfee 1977) have recently described a constant cuff pressure BP-biofeedback system which uses cuffs on each arm so that monitoring and feedback can be alternated from arm to arm and thus kept continual. With this device, they have obtained very good control of BP in normotensive subjects.

In our own laboratory, faced with the lack of technical expertise and funds to duplicate the Harvard group's BP-biofeedback system, we sought to circumvent these problems through developing a simplified, intermittent open-loop feedback system. In our system (Blanchard, Young, Haynes, and Kallman 1974d) the experimenter reads the BP value as it is automatically recorded on a polygraph once per minute. This value is plotted on a graph visible to the subject via closed-circuit television. Reliability checks show that rereading the polygraph record yields values within the limits of accuracy of the polygraph over 92 percent. The lag time from when the value is recorded to when it is plotted is about 4–5 seconds.

Using this feedback system we found that normotensives receiving feedback and instructions to increase BP could raise systolic BP significantly (about 3.5 mm Hg) over levels obtained without feedback (Blanchard *et al.* 1974d) which is comparable to the results obtained by the Harvard group. Moreover, when normotensives were asked to lower BP, subjects receiving this form of intermittent, analogue BP feedback lowered systolic BP significantly more than an instructed no-feedback group or a instructed binary feedback group across three separate daily sessions of 20 minutes each (decrease in BP of approximately 4 mm Hg).

In a final study we compared the use of this BP feedback system with a group taught to relax using EMG biofeedback and an instructed no-feedback control group (Blanchard, Haynes, Kallman, and Harkey 1976). Results showed that both feedback groups lowered BP significantly more than the no-feedback group but did not themselves differ. This leads one to suspect that the BP-biofeedback system we developed is only an elaborate means of teaching subjects to relax.

Clinical Applications

Unlike the work on clinical applications of HR biofeedback, the work in BP has centered on *one* problem, essential hypertension. The World Health Organization defines hypertension as BP in excess of 140 mm Hg, systolic, and/or in excess of 90 mm Hg, diastolic; approximately 90 percent of hypertension is classified as *essential hypertension,* or sustained elevated blood pressure for which no other physiological explanation is readily available. As noted previously, this disorder represents a major health problem in this country.

Direct feedback of blood pressure

In contrast to the clinical work with HR biofeedback, in BP applications the biological response for which biofeedback training is given is also the clinical response of interest. The first, and in some ways one of the best, study of BP feedback with hypertensive patients was conducted by the Harvard group using their BP biofeedback system (Benson, Shapiro, Tursky, and Schwartz 1971). Seven patients, all on stabilized doses of antihypertensive medication, were initially run in baseline sessions, during which time they sat comfortably relaxed, until their systolic BP measured in the session showed no further decrease for five consecutive sessions. Next BP-biofeedback training to lower systolic BP was begun and continued until the patient showed no further decrease over five consecutive sessions. Baseline and treatment phases were thus variable in length; averages for the entire group were approximately 11 baseline sessions and 22 treatment sessions.

Results showed that five of the seven patients showed marked (16 mm Hg or greater) decreases in systolic BP from end of baseline to end of treatment with an average decrease for all seven patients of 16.5 mm Hg. One patient was no longer in the hypertensive range at the end of baseline. Two of the six remaining hypertensive patients reduced their BP to within the normal range by the end of feedback training.

Two features of this study are especially praiseworthy: first, a very stable baseline was established prior to beginning treatment. The importance of this point is highlighted when one realizes that four of the seven patients required 15 or more sessions to reach stability. In our own work we have seen the BP of "apparently" hypertensive patients drop by 20 mm Hg or more over a series of baseline trials. Thus, especially in work with hypertensives, failure to obtain a stable baseline probably invalidates any study guilty of such failure. The second commendable feature is that five of seven patients showed marked reductions in BP.

The study's only shortcomings are in terms of experimental design. The failure to include a control group hinders clear-cut interpretation of the results since there is no control for attention-placebo factors. Moreover, the failure to return to baseline conditions to obtain follow-up data at the end leaves the study as a series of case studies rather than single-subject experiments. Informal follow-up (Benson 1975) revealed that the BP of all patients eventually returned to the hypertensive range. Regardless of its shortcomings, this study is one of the most frequently cited clinical applications of biofeedback training.

Schwartz and Shapiro (1973) conducted a similar study on a second group of seven hypertensive patients. There were several differences in the study: (1) based in part on their successful work with diastolic BP in normotensives (Shapiro *et al.* 1972), feedback of diastolic BP was used in the training; (2) patients were run for a fixed number of sessions in each condition. Unfortunately, there was no overall decrease in diastolic BP despite decreases within an individual session of up to 5 mm Hg. Although the results of this study are fairly discouraging, they are important because it is very helpful in the long run to know what does not work.

Comment. This study seemed to mark the end of the Harvard group's efforts at clinical studies of BP. Shapiro (1974) has reported on an additional hypertensive patient treated in his laboratory. Although the patient could show reductions in BP to 135/85 in the laboratory, his BP as measured by his physician was 160/110 both before and *after* treatment. Benson, likewise, found his hypertensives treated by biofeedback returned to their previously high levels of BP when he followed them up informally. Benson has apparently abandoned biofeedback and turned to use of the the "relaxation response" (Benson 1975), a meditative-like procedure, as a nonpharmacological treatment for hypertension.

Miller (1972) has reported on the successful biofeedback treatment of one case of hypertension. During a prolonged baseline (27 sessions) diastolic BP averaged 97 mm Hg. She was trained both to raise and lower BP using the apparatus from Miller's laboratory described earlier and could generate increases in BP of up to 20 mm Hg and decreases of up to 10 mm Hg. By the end of training, her diastolic BP had stabilized at about 76 mm Hg. This is even more impressive when one considers that during treatment she was withdrawn from antihypertensive medications (which should have increased her BP) and was discharged from the hospital (which typically would increase BP).

This represents an excellent systematic case study. However, one cannot rule out other factors as responsible for the changes because no control conditions were run. Miller, himself, noted that other factors may have been responsible for the changes.

Interestingly, in a later report Miller (1975b) noted that the patient "lost her voluntary control" of BP during a series of emotional crises and had to be restarted on antihypertensive drugs. Further biofeedback training led to some recovery of BP control. Miller (1975b) also reported that similar training procedures with over 20 other hypertensive patients had produced considerably poorer, not really promising, results. He too seems to have abandoned seeking to treat hypertensives with biofeedback.

One other important study (Kristt and Engel 1975) has been conducted using the Harvard group's constant cuff pressure apparatus on a very small sample ($n=5$). All five patients had ten-year documented histories of hypertension and all were on antihypertensive medications. At the start of the study all patients were taught to take their own BP at home; then for seven weeks prior to hospitalization all patients took their own BP four times daily and mailed these results to the investigators. Thus the study had a very stable baseline gathered in the patients' natural environment.

Next the patients were hospitalized for three weeks and taught to control BP through biofeedback training: for the first week, all subjects were taught to raise BP; then in the second week to lower BP; and in the final week to alternately raise and lower BP. Results in the hospital seem to demonstrate that patients did learn a certain degree of BP control, some more pronounced than others.

Most importantly, from both scientific and clinical points of view, all subjects continued to monitor BP at home and send in reports, and they also continued to practice lowering (without the complex biofeedback apparatus) at home. The important clinical results of this study are comparisons of baseline and posttreatment BP measured at home. Unfortunately baseline data were not available on one patient. For the other four, the decreases in systolic BP ranged from 9 to 36 mm Hg and averaged 18 mm Hg. For two of the patients significant decreases in diastolic BP (7 and 20 mm Hg, respectively) were found. Also three of the five patients were able to lower their antihypertensive medications.

These data present a possible strategy to teach true self-control of BP to hypertensive patients: intensive BP-biofeedback training followed by regular home practice and home monitoring to maintain the gains. Certainly these are the first data to give any kind of long-term follow-up of BP-biofeedback training. One could also speculate that merely teaching patients to monitor their own BP and letting them work on their own to discover psychological means to lower it will provide a practical strategy for dealing with elevated BP.

One controlled group outcome study has been completed in the area of BP biofeedback (Elder, Ruiz, Deabler, and Dillenkoffer 1973). After one baseline session, three groups of "hypertensive patients" ($n=6$) were run twice per day for a total of seven training sessions. One experimental group received only BP feedback and instructions to lower BP while a second group received both of these plus social reinforcement for success. A third group merely sat quietly and had BP monitored. Unlike the earlier work, BP was monitored and feedback was given only once every two minutes rather than beat by beat.

By the end of this brief treatment, the group receiving social reinforcement and BP biofeedback had lowered systolic BP by 15 percent and diastolic BP by over 20 percent. The latter change was significant and significantly lower than that obtained by the other two groups. The group receiving the BP biofeedback without the social reinforcement was significantly lower on diastolic BP by the end of training than the control group and had decreased by over 5 percent. Follow-up data collected one week later were essentially useless because of a large-scale differential dropout rate.

The lack of an adequate baseline robs this otherwise interesting study of much of its significance. Also there appear to be differences in the instructions given the two biofeedback groups. Finally it is hard to believe that social reinforcement (such things as telling the patient "good" or "you are doing well") can have such a pronounced effect on BP. Nevertheless, this study is certainly very provocative and warrants replication.

Elder and Eustis (1975) attempted a replication by running 22 hypertensive outpatients in their procedure combining BP biofeedback and social reinforcement. Although the training for most subjects was spread over a number of weeks, for four subjects ten training sessions were completed in two weeks. Overall, those patients receiving the massed training did better, lowering systolic BP by about 6 percent and diastolic BP by about 4 percent. Patients receiving the distributed training showed decreases of about 2–3 percent in both pressures. Considering all subjects together, systolic BP was reduced by about 8 mm Hg and diastolic BP by about 6 mm Hg. These results are certainly not as spectacular as those initially achieved by Elder *et al.* (1973) and fall in the range usually seen. It was certainly to his credit that Elder attempted the replication. Only further research will tell if the initial good results will hold up under repeated testing.

We have reported (Blanchard, Young, and Haynes 1975) from our laboratory on the treatment of four hypertensive patients in single-subject experiments using open-loop, intermittent visual feedback of BP. In each of the four instances systolic BP was lowered during the treatment phases to the normotensive range, decreases ranged from 9 to 51 mm Hg. The use of the single subject experimental design isolated the BP biofeedback as responsible for the decreases. Moreover, fairly stable baseline levels of BP were established before treatment was begun.

In all of our work we use 40-minute sessions: the first 15 minutes is an adaptation period; then follows a 5-minute, in-session baseline to determine the BP level for the subject for that day; next follows the BP biofeedback session in which the patient receives feedback 20 times at one-minute intervals. The results of this treatment for one male patient reported in Blanchard *et al.* (1975) are presented in Fig. 2.3. Each daily point represents the average of all 20 readings.

From inspecting Fig. 2.3, one can see that the baseline systolic BP averaged 142 mm Hg. Eight feedback trials led to a decrease in BP to 123 mm Hg. The return to baseline conditions for eight sessions did not lead to a return to previously high BP levels; instead BP seemed to have stabilized in a fashion similar to decreases in HR which have been reported; four additional biofeedback sessions, to

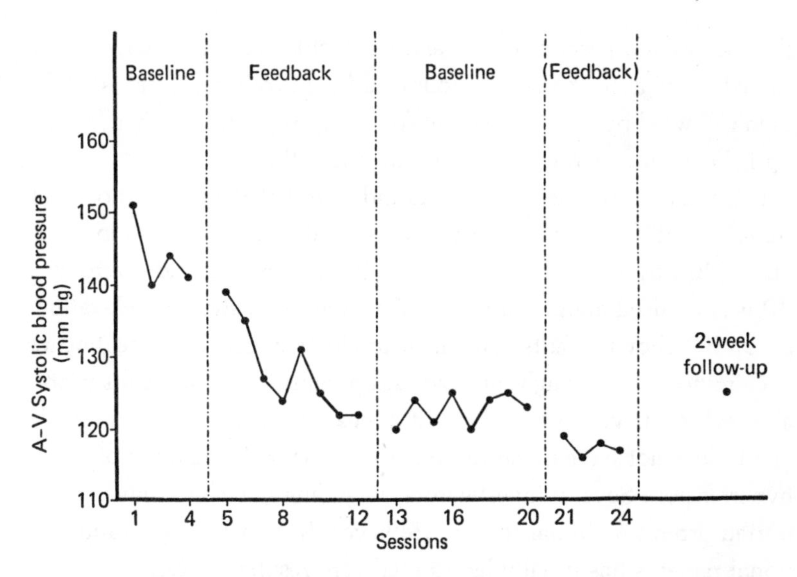

Fig. 2.3. Patient's average systolic blood pressure for each session of the experiment.

complete the A-B-A-B design, led to a further decrease in BP to an average value of 117 mm Hg. A follow-up at two weeks revealed that systolic BP was still low.

Since that time we have run a number of other hypertensive patients in our BP-feedback procedure with varying degrees of success, some patients achieving decreases of 10 to 20 mm Hg while others remain essentially unchanged.

Having frequently complained that controlled-group outcome studies were missing in this area (e.g., Blanchard and Young 1974; Blanchard *et al.* 1975), we decided to conduct one ourselves under a grant from the National Heart and Lung Institute. Patients diagnosed as suffering from essential hypertension by the physician consultant to the study were randomly assigned to one of three conditions: BP biofeedback of the intermittent, open-loop variety previously described, frontalis EMG feedback as a means of teaching relaxation, and a third group who were asked to try to relax themselves and practice this relaxation regularly. All patients received four baseline sessions, followed by 12 training sessions, and then followed by four immediate follow-up sessions. Further follow-up is being gathered over at least three months.

Preliminary analyses of the data indicate that there were no significant differences among the three treatment conditions in reducing BP. Systolic BP was reduced about 6 mm Hg and diastolic BP was reduced about 2 mm Hg. Thus the self-instructed relaxation group has shown results equivalent to either biofeedback treatment.

Comment. Although our own disappointing recent results probably color our view of the field, it appears to us that biofeedback of BP does not have much to offer to the general treatment of hypertension. Several investigators, including ourselves, have reported promising initial results. However, further testing in additional patients has usually led to mediocre results at best.

Three points do seem to emerge from these data, however: (1) more concentrated training, on a daily, or even twice-per-day, basis seems relatively more effective than training spread over several weeks. This is supported by the data from Benson *et al.* (1971), Elder *et al.* (1973), Elder and Eustis (1975), Kristt and Engel (1975) and even our own results. (2) Some patients seem to derive great benefit from BP-biofeedback training with large-scale reductions in BP. What is needed is a scheme to predict beforehand who is likely to benefit and who is not. Such a prediction scheme might be based on psychophysiological measures taken early in treatment. (3) Continued benefits from BP training seem to come primarily from continued monitoring of BP and continued regular practice once formal training is discontinued.

Other biofeedback treatment of hypertension

Although we stated in the beginning of this book that the chapters would be organized around the biological response for which biofeedback was given, in this section we are going to deviate from that organization by reviewing several studies in which the clinical response of interest is BP but the treatment is through biofeedback of other responses.

The best work in the area of the treatment of elevated BP through biofeedback and perhaps the best clinical work in all of biofeedback has been done by an Indian physician working in England, Dr. Chandra Patel. In her first study (Patel 1973) she treated 20 hypertensive patients with a combination of Western electronic technology and Eastern philosophy and religion. Patients, all but one of whom was on antihypertensive medication, attended three 30-minute sessions per week for three months and were given a combination biofeedback of galvanic skin resistance and passive relaxation training. In the latter patients were instructed to attend mentally to various parts of their bodies, to make them limp and relaxed, and then to focus attention on breathing. They were taught phrases similar to those from autogenic training (Schultz and Luthe 1969) and also similar to yoga exercises.

The biofeedback signal was a tone which increased in pitch as skin resistance increased. Supposedly this signal was directly related to sympathetic nervous system activity so that as the tone decreased in pitch, sympathetic arousal was reduced.

Results showed that 16 of 20 patients had decreases in BP. Systolic BP decreased an average of 25 mm Hg and diastolic 14 mm Hg. Five patients discontinued antihypertensive medications altogether and eight others had reductions of at least 33 percent.

These results were very impressive but were complicated by several experimental design issues: the lack of stable baseline data, lack of follow-up data, and most importantly, lack of a control group. Finally the experimenter did most of the BP measurements which is a possible source of bias.

The second study in the series (Patel 1975) answers several of these criticisms. This time two groups of 20 patients each, closely matched for age, sex, and initial BP, were selected. The experimental group received the same treatment as previously described: biofeedback of skin resistance and passive relaxation training akin to yoga. The control subjects came to the physician's office for the same number of visits and rested quietly in a reclining position. Experimental patients were instructed to practice the relaxation regularly during treatment and after it was concluded. Follow-up measurements were made at three, six, and twelve months.

Results showed highly significant ($p < 0.001$) decreases in the experimental patients for both systolic BP (20 mm Hg decrease) and diastolic BP (14 mm Hg decrease) with no change in the systolic BP of the control subjects and a small, nonsignificant decrease (2 mm Hg) in diastolic. The reductions in BP held up throughout the 12-month follow-up. Twelve patients were able to reduce medication level.

Thus this study answered three of the criticisms leveled at the first study: change in BP was calculated from data from the first three treatment sessions and thus constitutes a baseline; a control group which received equal attention was included; and a 12-month follow-up was obtained.

There remained only the issue of the experimenter being the one who made the BP readings. This was resolved in the third study (Patel and North 1975) which represents both a systematic replication and an extension of the earlier work.

Measurements of BP were made on three separate pretreatment visits for each member of a group of 34 hypertensive patients. Half ($n = 17$) were then randomly assigned to the treatment condition combining passive relaxation training, yoga, and biofeedback training, while the other half (controls) were seen for equal periods of time. Treatment time was reduced to twice weekly visits for six weeks. In the initial six sessions, biofeedback of skin resistance was given; in the later sessions EMG feedback from an unspecified site was used. Again experimental subjects were instructed to practice the relaxation twice per day and to try to incorporate relaxation into their daily life-style. Most importantly, all BP measurements were done by a nurse who was "blind" as to which condition a patient was in.

Results showed an average decrease in systolic BP of 26 mm Hg for the experimental subjects and 9 mm Hg for the controls and an average decrease in diastolic BP of 15 mm Hg for the experimental subjects and 4 mm Hg for the controls. These results represented significantly ($p<0.005$) greater reductions for the experimental subjects.

At the end of a three-month follow-up the BP of the experimental subjects had risen slightly: 84.4 to 87.9 diastolic and 141.4 to 148.8 systolic. Rises in the control group were substantially higher: 160.0 to 176.6 systolic and 96.4 to 104.3 diastolic. At this point Patel and North did a very important thing: they now treated the control subjects with the same procedure which had been used successfully with the experimental subjects. This action provides an exact replication of the treatment effect on a group who has previously not responded to repeated contact, attention, and periods of simple relaxation. Use of this "half-crossover" design is a very powerful technique.

The results of the second phase showed that the newly treated subjects experienced significant decreases in BP: 28 mm Hg systolic and 15 mm Hg diastolic. The subjects treated in the first half of the study maintained their lowered BP.

Comment. These three studies taken together seem to show conclusively that the combination of passive relaxation and meditation combined with biofeedback for lowered sympathetic arousal is very effective. They certainly represent a hallmark in the biofeedback literature. Only two questions remain: (1) Is biofeedback necessary for the success of the procedure? (2) Are the results replicable by another investigator?

Patel (personal communication 1976) seems to feel that the biofeedback aspect of her training regimen adds little. And as will be briefly outlined below, several others have provided data which concur in this notion.

There has been some work, as yet unpublished, which shows that EMG feedback training is useful in reducing the BP of hypertensive patients (Love, Montgomery, and Moeller 1974; Russ 1974). Moreover, Shoemaker and Tasto (1975) have shown that progressive relaxation training, modeled after that of Jacobson (1976), is useful in reducing BP.

Finally Herbert Benson and his colleagues have demonstrated in a series of studies (summarized in Benson's book, *The Relaxation Response*, 1975) that passive relaxation training combined with meditation can lead to significant reductions in BP for hypertensive patients. An interesting aspect of his work has been the finding that when patients discontinue the regular practice of eliciting the relaxation response their BP returns in about a month to pretreatment levels (Benson, Rosner, and Marzetta 1973). Thus in the treatment of hypertension by psychological means, as with the treatment through drugs, patient compliance may be a problem.

Comment. At this point it seems that BP biofeedback has not proved to be a reliably effective means of obtaining reductions in BP in hypertensive patients. Relaxation training, primarily of the passive-meditative type found in autogenic training, Transcendental Meditation, and the relaxation response, does seem to be effective. Certainly the combination of passive relaxation and skin resistance biofeedback developed by Patel seems to have held up under repeated experimental investigations of an ever more rigorous nature. A next logical step would be large-scale trials of these techniques in comparison with standard pharmacological treatment. It may be that compliance will be higher with the psychological treatment than with drug treatment because of a difference in side effects: with psychological treatment the side effects are usually positive and include a sense of relaxation and well-being; with drug treatment the side effects are frequently unpleasant and cause patients to discontinue treatment. Only further research will tell.

Peripheral Vascular Responses and Skin Surface Temperature

Whereas biofeedback research on control of heart rate and blood pressure began with basic research studies with normal subjects to define the parameters and later proceeded to the application of this knowledge about biofeedback techniques to clinical populations, the research on biofeedback with peripheral vascular responses *began* with clinical application. Only later has there been research on the basic mechanisms involved and on the parameters of the feedback process with normal subjects. In the late 1960s word began to spread from Topeka, Kansas, that workers (primarily Elmer and Alyce Green and Joseph Sargent) at the Menninger Clinic had discovered a psychological treatment for migraine headaches which involved biofeedback. It seems that during the course of some psychophysiological measurement studies on volunteers engaging in autogenic training, one woman demonstrated a large rise in hand temperature as she recovered from a migraine headache; she later was able to abort a headache by warming her hands. This serendipitous finding was partially confirmed through applying the thermal biofeedback training to several other volunteers among employees of the clinic who also suffered from migraine headaches. From this arose a new area of biofeedback research and application in the use of feedback of skin temperature.

Basic Research

Investigators recognized early that the vasomotor response (the degree of change in blood flow through a set of vessels, either reduction, that is, vasoconstriction, or increase, that is, vasodilation, is encompassed in the term vasomotor response) could provide a good system in which to demonstrate operant conditioning of autonomically mediated responses since the vasoconstriction response was thought to result from sympathetic arousal. Thus, even before the work of the Menninger group with migraine headaches appeared, Snyder and Noble (1968) reported on the "operant conditioning of vasoconstriction" in a group of normal subjects.

As blood flow in the fingers changes, several things happen: with decreased blood flow (vasoconstriction), the surface temperature decreases, the light-transmitting properties of the fingers change, and the actual size, or volume, of the fingers decreases. With vasodilation the opposite things occur. Snyder and Noble capitalized on the latter fact in their experiment. Two groups of subjects were "reinforced" or given feedback of success by a binary visual signal when they produced a vasoconstriction response. Control subjects received either no feedback or random feedback not related to their responses. The investigators took care to record, and hence control for, changes in forearm muscle tension (EMG) and respiration in order to rule out these voluntarily controlled responses as causing the observed changes. Their results clearly showed that the subjects given feedback for producing vasoconstrictions produced more such responses than the control subjects, thus showing that the vasoconstriction component of the vasomotor response could be brought under feedback control. This work was later replicated by Stern and Pavloski (1974).

The remainder of the basic research has used measurement and feedback of skin temperature as a means of studying the vasomotor response. Taub and Emurian (1973) reported on the successful demonstration of hand temperature changes in normal subjects using analogue visual feedback. Attempts to replicate these findings have met with some difficulties, however.

Lynch, Hama, Kohn, and Miller (1974) reported on an unsuccessful attempt to replicate the results of Taub and Emurian. Despite giving subjects extensive thermal biofeedback training (18 daily 15-minute sessions) very little evidence of temperature increase was found. Some subjects did show evidence of cooling the hands, or vasoconstriction. These investigators next ran 100 subjects in a single training session to test the generality of the ability. Fourteen subjects could demonstrate cooling on the first trial; however, only three of these could repeat it on a second day. One of the latter subjects could reliably show large changes on repeated trials.

In later work, this same team (Lynch, Hama, Kohn, and Miller 1976), working with children, was able to demonstrate good control of vasomotor responding. In a fairly strenuous test of vasomotor control, the subjects were asked to change the temperature of one hand relative to the other hand. Three of the four subjects learned, with the aid of the biofeedback training, to do this producing differences of 2° to 3°C between the hands. One child could even produce small (1.2°C) but reliable differences in temperature between two fingers on the same hand!

Surwit and his associates (Surwit, Shapiro, and Feld 1976), in a well-controlled study, sought to determine if normal subjects could learn to control hand temperature with the aid of biofeedback and then to determine the vascular mechanisms involved. Temperature was recorded from both hands as well as measures of blood flow, respiration, and HR. Training was for five or nine sessions after two baseline sessions and was conducted in a chamber in which ambient temperature was controlled precisely.

Results showed that subjects readily learned to decrease hand temperature by an average of 2°C, with one subject showing a decrease of 10°C. However, subjects trained to increase hand temperature showed only slight changes over baseline, averaging an increase of only 0.25°C. Although feedback was from only one hand, the observed changes occurred readily in both hands.

In a second study, the room temperature was lowered so that the new subjects' starting point or baseline surface temperature would be lower. The reason for this is that in the first study, baseline temperature was within 2°C of basal body temperature (35.9°C). The result of this second study was *poorer* performance of subjects trying to increase hand temperature and a failure to show any increase over trials. This means that the initial small degree of increase was *not* due to a ceiling effect.

The overall conclusions from the work of Surwit *et al.* (1976) as well as that from Lynch *et al.* (1976) is that temperature decreases (vasoconstriction) are fairly easy for normal subjects to learn with biofeedback training, but that temperature increases (vasodilation) are difficult and that the increases obtained are typically of low magnitude. Keefe (1975) and Gardner and Keefe (1976) have presented data slightly at odds with this conclusion. In both studies, with extended (12 sessions) training, subjects trained to increase finger temperature were significantly higher than subjects trained to lower it, even when they had not been informed of the response. Changes in either direction averaged only about 1°C (1.5 to 2.0°F).

Comment. This finding that the response associated with sympathetic arousal (vasoconstriction) is easier to produce in normals than the opposite one is analogous to the results of HR biofeedback training in normals. It would seem that only subjects whose basal state is much removed from the normal baseline can produce either large scale decreases in HR or large scale increases in finger temperature. We also see another example in which most of the basic research is on the response (vasoconstriction) which has the least clinical utility.

Hypnosis, biofeedback, and skin temperature

An additional line of research in this area was recently introduced by Maslach, Marshall, and Zimbardo (1972). Working both with hypnotized and nonhypnotized, but highly motivated subjects, Maslach *et al.* were able to demonstrate consistent changes in the temperature of the two hands in the hypnotized subjects through hypnotic suggestion (average difference of about 4°C) but no differences in the nonhypnotized controls. In general the differences were due to large decreases in the "cold" hand (up to 7°C) with relatively small increases in the warm hand (up to 2°C).

Roberts, Kewman, and MacDonald (1973) replicated these results in a study of six subjects who had high hypnotic susceptibility and much prior hypnotic training. These subjects were given biofeedback training while in a hypnotic trance. Five of the six could produce reliable and statistically significant differences in temperature between the two hands. The magnitude of difference ranged from about 0.3°C to about 3.0°C. On some trials, the two best subjects could produce differences of 3.7°C and 9.2°C, and continued to be able to make large changes even after feedback was removed. It is not clear from the report whether the differences were due to increasing the temperature of one hand or decreasing the temperature in the nontargeted hand, or both. In any event, in a certain select proportion of the population, the ability to control skin temperature with feedback training is fairly dramatic. Whether or not this has value for the clinical populations is the subject of the next sections.

Clinical Applications

Migraine headaches

Migraine, or vascular, headaches were first described by the ancient Greeks. They are characterized as being predominantly one-sided (although in later stages of the headache the pain may be described as on both sides of the head), episodic, and intermittent, preceded upon occasion by an aura or prodromal symptoms which let the patient know the headache is coming, and lasting from several hours to a few days. Moreover, the headache is *extremely painful.* Anyone who has not suffered migraine headaches cannot usually conceive of the pain and misery which the throbbing headaches inflict upon migraine victims. For some of these unfortunates, the only solution is to retire to a quiet, darkened room and suffer through the nausea and pain. For others, vasodilating drugs such as the ergotamines or strong analgesics, such as codeine, provide some relief. Not infrequently migraine sufferers also have muscle contraction or tension headaches but can clearly tell the difference in the two types of headaches. One can frequently find that other family members have migraine headaches: we have found three-generation family histories upon occasion.

Given such a widespread and debilitating disorder, it is no wonder that the early informal reports from the Menninger group received an enthusiastic welcome. Unfortunately, the first formal report on their results (Sargent, Green, and Walters 1972) left much to be desired in terms of experimental design.

In their initial work Sargent *et al.* (1972) combined autogenic training (originated by Schultz and Luthe 1969) in which the patient learns to repeat certain key autogenic phrases such as, "I feel quiet . . . I am beginning to feel quite relaxed," and later, "My hands are warm . . . ," with biofeedback training and regular home practice in both. In their initial work, temperature was monitored from both the fingertip and forehead; feedback was given of the difference in temperature between the two sites with the instruction to warm the hands relative to the forehead. Laboratory training sessions took place once per week and were supplemented by home practice with a portable biofeedback device.

Of the 75 patients studied, the authors were able to confirm improvement in 29 percent to 39 percent of the sample. The data gathering was far from systematic, and the authors acknowledged that a lack of baseline data, a high degree of variability in their data, and lack of agreement among the raters prevented standard statistical analyses of their data.

Although the study represents only an anecdotal case report because of design flaws, it was *highly influential* in the biofeedback world as judged by the proliferation of temperature-training devices and reports on treatment of migraine patients.

The Menninger group (Sargent, Green, and Walters 1973) have presented a second report on their work involving 28 patients, 20 of whom had definite migraine headaches, two with "questionable migraine" attacks, and six with tension, or muscle contraction, headaches. It is not clear whether these were new patients or some of the original 75 described in the first report.

The results of this study show 12 of 19 (63 percent) migraine patients as definitely improved based on clinical evaluation and the patients' daily records of headache intensity and medication use. Two of the six patients with tension headaches were improved; one migraine patient was unaccounted for.

This study, although lacking many desirable control features, does provide more systematic data on the outcome of the thermal biofeedback training than the first report. However, the lack of adequate baseline data, and more importantly, the lack of any control for expectancy, or attention-placebo effects seriously limits the value of the study as scientific data.

Coincident with or following these initial reports, several other investigators have reported on the use of temperature-biofeedback training with migraine headache patients. Wickramasekera (1973a) reported on the treatment of two patients with migraine headaches who were treated in such a fashion that some of the attention-placebo effects were controlled. Both patients had long histories of migraine headaches which had been unresponsive to medication and traditional verbal psychotherapy. Most importantly, both received rather lengthy courses of frontalis EMG biofeedback training (16 and 18 sessions, respectively) with no relief. This phase of treatment controls to some extent for expectancy effects in the thermal biofeedback treatment.

After a three-week, no-treatment phase, during which headache intensity and frequency data were gathered as well as data on medication usage, differential temperature training like that of the Menninger group was instituted on a once per week basis. Within three to four weeks the patients had mastered the hand-warming response, and headache frequency and intensity began to decrease.

By the eleventh week headache activity was essentially absent in one patient and at very low levels in the other. These two systematic case studies provide fairly strong evidence of the value of the biofeedback training since the autogenic training was omitted and since they had not responded to other biofeedback training.

Recently, Turin and Johnson (1976) reported on the treatment of seven migraine patients with thermal biofeedback alone. After a baseline period of four to six weeks during which patients began keeping records of medication use and headache activity, they were given twice weekly biofeedback-training sessions in which temperature feedback was only from the fingertip (instead of the differential temperature training introduced by the Menninger group), the autogenic training was omitted, and home practice was without the benefit of a biofeedback device. The training lasted for 14 weeks.

Results showed significant reduction in headache frequency and medication consumption on a group basis. Fortunately individual data were presented. An examination of these showed that only three, and possibly four, patients made a large scale, clinically meaningful, improvement (headache frequency reduced by 50 percent, medication reduced by 50 percent) and these patients showed a better hand-warming response.

This single group study adds to the mounting evidence that there may really be something to the temperature biofeedback training which is therapeutic for migraine headaches. However, in the final analysis, only a controlled group-outcome study can confirm the efficacy of a procedure. We have recently completed such a study at Memphis State University (Blanchard, Theobald, Brown, Silver, and Williamson 1977).

Over 150 people responded to newspaper and television advertisements for migraine headache sufferers. After an initial telephone screening, 77 were further screened through personal interviews; 39 met our specific inclusion and exclusion criteria which included at least one migraine headache per month, predominantly one-sided headaches accompanied usually by nausea and photophobia, and a confirmatory diagnosis by their personal physician of migraine or vascular headache.

These patients were put through a four-week baseline during which they recorded headache intensity on a five-point scale four times per day as well as recording information on medication usage. At the end of baseline, 37 patients remained. They were then formed into matched trios and randomly assigned to one of three conditions: (1) a combination of temperature biofeedback, autogenic training and regular home practice; (2) a combination of progressive relaxation with regular home practice; and (3) a no-treatment, waiting-list control condition. Treatment consisted of twice per week training sessions for six weeks; each of three experimenters saw approximately one-third of the subjects in each condition.

Thirty subjects (10 per condition) finished the training. Early dropouts from each of the two treatment conditions were replaced by patients from the waiting list. Two others were not. Three patients from the waiting-list condition dropped out or moved.

Results based on a comparison of the last two weeks of treatment with baseline data showed that all three groups had decreased frequency of headaches. The two treated groups had significant reductions in total headache activity (average of the four daily headache intensity ratings, see Fig. 2.4), peak headache intensity, and medication usage whereas the waiting-list group did not change significantly on the latter three measures. Most importantly, there were no differences between the two treated groups on any dependent measure. Thus treatment by standard progressive relaxation training was equally as effective as thermal biofeedback training supplemented with autogenic training.

Those patients on the waiting list who desired treatment ($n = 6$) were randomly split between thermal biofeedback and relaxation training. The addition of their posttreatment data did not change the results.

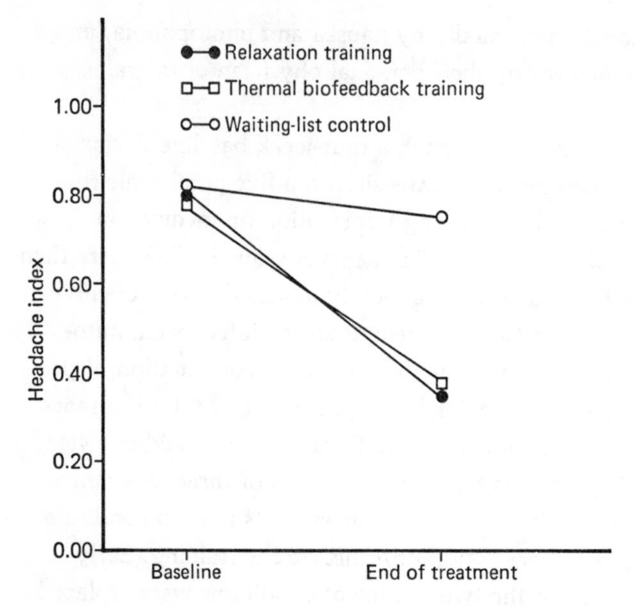

Fig. 2.4. Changes in headache index for all three experimental groups as a result of treatment.

Follow-up data revealed an interesting phenomena: those patients who continued to practice either the relaxation training or the autogenic training and hand-warming response regularly maintained their reductions in headache activity. Those who began to skip the practice experienced a return of the headache activity.

Taking all of the indices plus clinical interview data into account, approximately 60 percent of each treated group was much improved at the end of treatment, 20 percent was somewhat improved, and 20 percent was relatively unimproved.

Mitchell and Mitchell (1971) have reported similar improvement in patients with migraine headaches who were treated with behavioral therapy including relaxation training. Lutker (1971) has also reported on a single case of migraine headache in which the patient did not respond to a variety of medications but did get long-lasting relief with relaxation training similar to that used in the Blanchard *et al.* study.

Comment. At this point it seems fairly well established that thermal biofeedback training and regular home practice of the hand-warming response leads to marked improvement in a substantial proportion (50 to 75 percent) migraine sufferers. However, a similar proportion of migraine sufferers also respond to relaxation training with regular home practice. Boudewyns (1976) has shown that fingertip temperature tends to increase when normal subjects are given relaxation training and decreases under stress. It may be that the final common pathway of action in migraine for both relaxation training and biofeedback training is a relaxation response which includes peripheral vasodilation and hence skin temperature increase.

At this point, no one knows if a combination of thermal biofeedback and relaxation training would be more effective than either alone since one method might work for patients for whom the other method is ineffective. Only further research will tell.

It is known that the external arteries of the head undergo vasomotor changes during the various stages of a migraine attack (Wolff 1963). In the early or prodromal stage, there is evidence for vasoconstriction; later during the initial stages of the headache, when the pain is most severe, there is evidence for extreme vasodilation. The pain itself supposedly comes from the activation of the nerve fibers surrounding the dilated arteries. In the final stages, the artery remains relatively dilated and edematous.

At this point no one has shown why dilating the blood vessels of the hands has any effect on the vasomotor tone of the cranial blood vessels. It is assumed to be through some form of sympathetic nervous system mediation but the actual mechanism is unclear.

Direct training to control cranial vasomotor activity

Several investigators have sought to attack migraine headache more directly by training patients to control the vasomotor activity of the cephalic blood vessels, particularly the temporal artery. Koppman, McDonald, and Kunzel (1974) were able to demonstrate control of relative size of the temporal artery in migraine patients using the amplitude of the blood volume pulse as the biological response and giving feedback as they learned to alternately dilate and constrict it. In a more elaborate study Friar and Beatty (1976) used multisite recording and an on-line computer to teach patients with frequent migraine headaches to decrease the amplitude of the pulse in the temporal artery. After eight training sessions, the experimental group in a ninth no-feedback session could reduce pulse amplitude to 80 percent of that seen prior to training and significantly greater than that of subjects trained to reduce hand pulse amplitude. Thus voluntary cranial vasoconstriction was learned. The patients were instructed to practice the response in an attempt to abort headaches. Results of a 30-day trial showed that the experimental subjects had significantly fewer major headache attacks than did the controls. However, headache intensity and medication use were not significantly reduced.

Finally, Feuerstein and Adams (1975) presented data on several migraine patients who were treated with cephalic vasomotor (CVM) feedback. Although there was some evidence of learning to reduce the CVM response, the beneficial effects for the migraine patients were not impressive, and were not statistically significant within single subjects.

Comment. At this point research on direct biofeedback of cephalic vasomotor activity has not shown any strong clinical effects. It is certainly more cumbersome than the thermal biofeedback but does seem to make sense physiologically. Only later research will tell if it offers any advantage over thermal biofeedback or relaxation training.

Raynaud's disease

Raynaud's disease is a functional disorder of the peripheral vascular system in which the patient suffers from painful episodes of vasoconstriction in the hands, and sometimes the feet. During an attack the skin blanches and is cold to the touch. Attacks are usually precipitated either by exposure to cold, such as touching a cold doorknob barehanded, or by emotional upset. In severe cases, minor cuts and sores do not readily heal because of insufficient blood supply, and gangrene can develop.

Treatment has traditionally consisted of keeping the extremities warm and well protected in cold weather as well as by supplying external warmth during an attack. Drugs help sometimes. In some cases surgery is performed to cut the neural connections from the sympathetic nervous system (sympathectomy) to the extremities.

With the advent of biofeedback training both for skin temperature and peripheral vasomotor activity, it was inevitable that someone would try to treat this relatively rare condition with biofeedback. Schwartz (1972b) reported on two cases of Raynaud's disease using biofeedback training of blood volume. In the successful case, a man with Raynaud's in the feet learned to increase blood volume in the big toe in ten training sessions. The patient remained symptom free for a year and half and then returned for "booster" treatments. Interestingly, he claimed to have developed certain imagery which enabled him to warm his feet on his own away from treatment. The other case was a woman with Raynaud's disease of the hands. She dropped out of treatment after fewer than ten sessions and showed no evidence of learning to control the biological response or of symptomatic relief.

Surwit (1973) has provided a detailed case study of a female patient with Raynaud's whose treatment included temperature-biofeedback training among other things. The patient had already had two sympathectomies in an effort to relieve the disorder. During the six months of treatment she received over 50 thermal-biofeedback training sessions. Her basal skin temperature increased from 23.0 to 26.6°C and she showed other marked clinical improvement. However, the patient "lost" her ability to control her hand temperature shortly after treatment ended.

Jacobson, Hackett, Surman, and Silverberg (1973) treated a male with a three-year history of Raynaud's which had not responded to medication. Initially treatment was through hypnosis and suggestions of warmth but this yielded little change over three sessions. During five thermal-biofeedback training sessions the patient rapidly learned to increase fingertip temperature by approximately 4°C. This ability was accompanied by clinical improvement which was maintained at a follow-up seven months later.

All of the reports above represent either anecdotal case reports of systematic case studies in terms of level of sophistication of the experimental design (Blanchard and Young 1974). In a study completed in our laboratory the level of sophistication was moved one step higher through the use of a single-subject experiment (Blanchard and Haynes 1975). After establishing a baseline of basal skin temperature of the hand, the patient, a young woman with a mild to moderate case of Raynaud's, was given blocks of sessions in which she was instructed to try to raise hand temperature (A) alternated with blocks in which the same instructions were given as well as biofeedback of the difference in hand temperature and forehead temperature (B).

Results showed a clear-cut advantage for feedback sessions over instructed, no-feedback sessions. Follow-up sessions were held at two, four, and seven months and included both self-control and feedback-assisted-control sessions. Ability to generate an increase in hand temperature of at least 2°F was always readily reestablished. Most importantly, the patient showed an increase in basal hand temperature, measured at the beginning of each session, of 12°F from the initial baseline sessions to the end of training. At the follow-ups, basal temperature remained at least 7.8°F higher than the initial value. Clinically the patient reported that she was much improved and that she had learned to generate a feeling of warmth in her hands, and sometimes her feet, through certain self-instructions and imagery. The latter is reminiscent of Schwartz's (1972b) successful case and a good illustration of generalization to the patient's natural environment.

Since these reports have appeared, several other successful cases of treatment of Raynaud's disease with thermal biofeedback have been reported including a series of three cases by Sedlacek (1976) and eight cases by May and Weber (1976). In the latter *all* patients could show at least a 2°C increase in hand temperature after 16 training sessions and average number of painful vasospastic episodes were reduced from 5/wk to 1/wk.

Comment. At this point reports have appeared in which at least 22 cases of Raynaud's disease have been treated with some form of biofeedback training. Of these, at least 20 were somewhat successful. It would certainly seem that, with such a success rate (which may be somewhat inflated because it is easier to publish successful cases than unsuccessful ones), biofeedback training should be the treatment of choice. At the very minimum, it should be tried before the patient undergoes a surgical sympathectomy since that is irreversible.

What is needed is a small-scale controlled group-outcome study in this area. Also it would be helpful to learn if biofeedback of vasomotor response would be more efficacious than thermal biofeedback since the former attacks the problem more directly. A final interesting point is that these patients, who typically have low basal skin temperatures, seem to acquire a large-magnitude hand-warming response fairly readily as contrasted with the difficulty in showing such a response in normals. This seems to be another example, similar to HR lowering, of being able to show a large-magnitude response only in a clinical population in which the baseline is abnormal and the training is prolonged.

3

Muscular Responses

Physiological Basis for the Electromyogram

Previous reviews of clinical biofeedback (Blanchard and Young 1974; Blanchard and Epstein 1977) have indicated the work done with muscle activity is some of the most consistent and clinically useful in biofeedback. The predominant technique for measurement of the physiological, as opposed to motoric, aspects of muscular responses is the electromyogram, or EMG.

Muscles are made up of numerous muscle fibers bound together by connective tissue. Individual fibers are very thin (0.1 mm wide) with varying lengths of up to 310 mm (Basmajian 1976). The number and size of fibers that constitute a muscle will vary depending on the size and function of the muscle.

When a muscle fiber is stimulated, it contracts to as little as 57 percent of resting length (Haines 1932, 1934). During muscle contraction all the fibers within the muscle do not operate as one unit, instead some contract while others do not. Fibers are grouped into functional units called *motor units.* All fibers in a motor unit will contract almost simultaneously because the fibers in an individual motor unit are connected by the terminal branches of a single nerve fiber. The nerves are connected to the muscle fibers at motor endplates located at the midpoint of the muscle.

The innervation for the impulse that causes a motor unit to fire are in the spinal cord or brainstem. A neural impulse traveling to a motor unit will produce contraction of all the fibers served by that nerve. The number of motor units that are activated is a function of the degree of contraction of the muscle, with an increase in units accompanying greater contractions. The summation of the electrical activity of numerous motor units in a muscle will produce apparently smooth overt muscle movement.

When a muscle fiber is activated, a wave of excitation electrical in nature spreads along the fiber. This electrical activity is the basis for fiber contraction.

Measurement of the EMG

The basis for the electromyogram is the detection of the electrical muscle action potentials (MAP) produced when the muscle contracts. When electrodes are placed along a muscle fiber, the changes in electrical potentials along the fiber can be detected, and then amplified and displayed. The detection can involve either the use of surface electrodes placed on the skin or needle electrodes placed directly in the muscle. If surface electrodes are used, the electrical activity detected is a product of the activity of the summation of numerous motor units, and the electrical signal detected is that which diffuses from the muscles through tissues to the skin. Thus, the measurement of whole muscles or muscle groups can be accomplished by using surface electrodes. Electrodes that are placed directly in the muscle can be used to greater advantage when measurement of the specific activity of an individual motor unit is desired. This is the case in much clinical electromyography, where the functional characteristics of motor units are studied.

Display and Reduction of the EMG

After the EMG has been detected, it is amplified and then displayed. An important question in research using the EMG is how to reduce all of the electrical activity recorded to a signal which is both meaningful and representative of all of the ongoing activity. This is particularly a problem with the EMG because of the very high frequency of the response; in electromyography there is the possibility of hundreds of individual MAPs being generated each second.

There are three ways to display the EMG, each of which has particular advantages for data reduction. The first technique is simply to display the raw EMG signal. The display device must be capable of accurately presenting responses that occur very quickly. This is best performed by an oscilloscope. Permanent records of oscilloscope tracings are possible by taking photographs of the oscilloscope screen. Most researchers agree that pen-writing galvonometers may not respond fast enough to represent accurately individual motor unit changes. However, gross differences in activity levels are easily observed with pen-writing systems.

Of the measures available from the raw EMG, two will be presented. First, the maximum amount of electricity generated by the contraction of muscle, scored by measuring the largest muscle action potential over a short period of time (like once per second) can be obtained. This information might be useful in quantifying change in muscle strength as a function of muscle retraining in stroke patients. The second measure is more representative of activity over time, rather than for a short trial. This consists of counting the number of muscle action potentials produced by a muscle that exceed a certain minimum criterion electrical level. For example, one could assess differences in resting levels over time in a spastic muscle achieved through two different procedures designed to reduce spasticity by counting all potential greater than 5 microvolts.

A second way to reduce EMG data is to use an average, or leaky, integrator (Shaw 1967). This device provides an electrical signal that is an analogue of the raw signal, such that variations in the frequency and amplitude of the raw signal are reflected in changes in the average tracing. The average integrator may process the signal at a rapid rate, such that the average signal appears similar to the unintegrated record, or the integrator can process the signal at a slower rate, so only large variations in the raw signal produce changes in the average signal. The average analogue signal is best used to detect changes in EMG levels over time, and typically is time sampled, or scored at regular time intervals. The best representation of ongoing activity is obtained by frequent sampling of the average signal (Epstein and Webster 1975), as often as once every four seconds.

The third technique produces the best estimates of EMG levels over time. It is called cumulative integration, and operates such that all the activity in a certain time period is added together. During calibration, the continuous EMG level necessary to produce various cumulative activity levels can be determined, so that the cumulated value during measurement can be quickly converted to the amount of muscle activity that is required over a specific time interval to produce the cumulative amount of activity observed.

The typical time interval is one second, such that cumulative records can be converted to microvolt/seconds, which is the amount of electrical activity necessary to be generated by a muscle in a second to produce a certain amount of cumulated activity. Smaller sampling periods will result in better estimates of ongoing changes than long sample intervals.

Basic Research

Single motor units

Research in this section will cover experiments designed to assess control of single motor units, or groups of a few units. As previously described, a single motor unit is the smallest functional unit of a muscle, and control of individual units is one of the most specific and remarkable effects in biofeedback. While few observers would be impressed with observing a subject move the arm on command, a task which involves recruiting many scores of motor units from various muscles, it is impressive when subjects are trained to isolate the firing of one motor unit in a muscle or to regulate the rate of firing of this motor unit while suppressing the firing of other surrounding units.

An early example of single motor unit control was reported by Lindsley (1935). In the process of studying the characteristics of single motor unit activity during voluntary contraction, Lindsley found that most subjects could completely relax a muscle when instructed to the point that no motor unit firing could be observed.

Hefferline and his colleagues then performed two interesting studies on small thumb muscle contractions ("thumb twitches") which involved no overt thumb movement. In a first study, Hefferline, Keenan, and Harford (1959) showed that the rate of the thumb twitch could become a function of escape and avoidance contingencies, such that the small muscle responses could postpone aversive noise programmed according to a Sidman avoidance schedule. Hefferline and Perera (1963) then showed that the small muscle response could also serve as a discriminative stimulus by arranging for a subject to be reinforced if the subject made an overt key press response after the thumb response.

In the first study using feedback to influence single motor unit activity Harrison and Mortensen (1962) demonstrated that subjects could be trained to produce contractions of individual motor units in the tibialis anterior muscle (the leg muscle next to the shin bone) with the aid of auditory and visual cues. In 1963 Basmajian (1963a, 1963b) published two papers describing his initial attempts to train subjects to control single motor unit activity through the use of auditory feedback. The simplicity of the auditory feedback used in most of the single motor unit control studies deserves note: it was simply the amplification of the muscle action potentials into a loudspeaker. In these first two reports, Basmajian indicated each of 16 subjects were readily trained to contract single motor units in the thumb (abductor pollicis brevis). They could also vary the rate of firing of the single motor units. As subjects were able to reliably control the rate of contractions of the motor unit, they were able to produce rhythmic patterns of firing, producing even "complicated drumrolls and drumbeats with internal rhythms" (Basmajian 1963a, 1963b). Also, many subjects were able to gain control over more than one motor unit and reportedly maintained the control after feedback was stopped.

Concurrent with Basmajian's work, Carlsöö and Edfeldt (1963) published reports in Sweden of single motor unit control of the first dorsal interosseous muscle. Their experiments suggested that auditory feedback was superior to visual feedback. Wagman, Pierce, and Burger (1965) replicated these results for several different muscles, and again indicated the superiority of auditory versus visual feedback. They also suggested that the control of some single motor units may be influenced by positions of the adjacent joint. Basmajian later replicated his procedures on more subjects (Basmajian, Baeza, and Fabrigar 1965). He also reported (Simard and Basmajian 1967) maintenance of control without feedback for the tibialis anterior muscle.

The single motor control technology has also been extended to children. Fruhling, Basmajian, and Simard (1969) reported control of hand, neck, and back muscles in a sample of 12 normal children, two years, five months to five years of age. Simard (1969) presented a very extensive analysis of EMG control in children, analyzing control of the rhomboid (back) muscle in 51 children 2½ to 12 years of age. Two levels of control were observed. All of the children were able to achieve some gross control of muscle contractions and relaxation. Ninety percent were also able to demonstrate single motor unit control, and about one-half of the sample were able to control single motor unit firing while engaged in drinking, an activity involving muscles in the opposite upper extremity.

Lloyd and Leibrecht have performed two studies analyzing the process of learning single motor unit control. In an initial investigation Lloyd and Leibrecht (1971) evaluated tibialis anterior muscle control in 17 subjects as a function of binary visual feedback. Each of the subjects was tested on two occasions to assess the effects of reexposure to the training procedures. Their results indicated isolation and control of single motor units in 13 of the 17 subjects, with 14 demonstrating control during the second testing session. Of major interest was the significantly better performance of the subjects during the initial trials of the second session as compared with the initial trials of the first session indicating some relatively permanent transfer, or learning. No differences in performance were observed across sessions for the terminal training trials of the two sessions. Leibrecht, Lloyd, and Pounder (1973) extended this work by testing subjects under similar conditions with the addition of auditory feedback in the initial test. No auditory feedback was available during the second test. Results indicated better acquisition of control as a function of auditory plus visual feedback than previously observed for visual feedback alone (Lloyd and Leibrecht 1971). However, the retesting data were very similar to that observed when visual feedback alone was used. These results indicate better acquisition of control, but no better maintenance of control, as a function of providing subjects with auditory plus visual feedback.

The specificity of control of single motor units has also been studied by Basmajian. Basmajian and Simard (1967) trained subjects to isolate and contract the right tibialis anterior muscle, and evaluated the effects of left lower extremity movement, right upper extremity movement, and positioning of the movement of proximal, crossed, and distal lower extremity joints on right tibialis anterior control. Results generally demonstrated single motor unit control during these concurrent activities and distractions.

Although subjects can control single motor units during additional sensory stimulation, Lloyd and Shurley (1976) showed that a reduction in sensory stimulation did improve single motor unit control of the tibialis anterior muscle. Twenty subjects were exposed to an initial session of single motor unit control with auditory feedback in a nonisolated or sensory/perceptual isolated environment. During the second session half the subjects who had been exposed to each of the two environments were now exposed to training in the other environment, while the other half remained in their original training settings. During the first session, the isolated subjects acquired the response faster than ones not isolated. Results for the second session showed best acquisition for the subjects provided isolation on both occasions, with the group receiving no isolation on either occasion showing the poorest acquisition. Subjects going from nonisolated to isolated environments showed an improvement in acquisition during the second session. Their performance was very similar to isolated subjects who were nonisolated on the second session, since these latter subjects showed a slight decrement in performance.

Petajan and Phillip (1969) analyzed the degree of single motor unit control across various muscle groups. Subjects were instructed to identify a single motor unit and regulate the rate of firing, gradually increasing the rate until a second motor unit action potential was observed, and then to maintain the rate of firing of the first unit. Three measures of motor unit control were analyzed across 16 muscles. These measures were the onset interval, calculated by establishing the longest stable interspike interval between control of one single motor unit to recruitment of a second unit; the recruitment interval, which was the time interval preceding the decrease in firing of the first unit after the second unit was recruited, and a range of control estimate, established by subtracting the onset interval from the recruitment interval, and dividing that by the recruitment interval. Results indicated single motor unit control was observed across each of the 16 muscles studied, with the most precise control in the frontalis, and the least precise in the biceps femoris. In general, facial muscles were controlled better than upper or lower extremity muscles.

The reports of single motor unit control have indicated success across the majority of subjects studied. However, there may be individual differences that influence the acquisition of single motor unit control. Scully and Basmajian (1969) studied the acquisition of single motor units control in 13 manually skilled and 16 unskilled subjects. The results indicated the manually skilled required more time to learn to control a hand (abductor digiti minimi) muscle than the unskilled. Zappalá (1970) studied single motor unit control of the tibialis anterior as a function of sex and knowledge of muscle anatomy and physiology as well as of electromyography. Subjects were exposed to training for a two- to four-hour session. Results showed that males are somewhat better at this task than females, and that knowledge about muscles and electromyography also was useful in facilitating control.

Single motor unit control has been replicated over many muscle groups in various labs. Basmajian (1967a, 1972) has updated his reviews of single motor unit control, as well as attempting to standardize testing and training procedures (Basmajian and Sampson 1973), to make comparisons of results across laboratories easier. He has recommended standards for types of feedback, subject-experimenter interactions, types of training tasks, and arrangement of work and rest intervals. Basmajian also has designed and validated a portable EMG device (Kukulka and Basmajian 1975) providing binary audio and visual feedback. This device could be used by the therapists in the field or patients at home.

Johnson (1976) has attempted to identify which of the standard tasks mentioned by Basmajian are best related to single motor unit control. He did this by correlating errors in the five tasks; (1) relaxing the muscle, (2) isolating a single motor unit, (3) controlling the rate of firing, (4) regulating the onset and offset of regular firing, and (5) producing rhythmic firing at the rate of one per second, with the total control score. The correlation analysis indicated tasks 2, 4, and 5 were most predictive of overall control. Johnson suggests minimal attention be paid to tasks 1 and 3.

Summary

This single motor unit research represents some of the most powerful effects of biofeedback procedures on bodily functions. The studies demonstrate reliable control of single motor units in numerous labs across numerous muscles, with consistent reports of the superiority of auditory to visual feedback. Subsequent to the numerous anecdotal demonstrations of the early phenomena, the quality of the research methodology has steadily improved. However, in few of the studies has adequate attention been paid to appropriate controls, necessary to analyze the process of the observed conditioning.

Analogue Studies

The studies of control of single motor units served as the basis for much of the use of EMG biofeedback in clinical work. In fact, the reader may be able to anticipate some of the uses of EMG control for stuttering or tension headaches. However, before the clinical literature is surveyed, it may be useful to survey the analogue research on EMG control. These studies are done with normal subjects, and they are usually designed to test assumptions on which clinical use of EMG biofeedback are based.

An early analogue EMG biofeedback study was performed by Budzynski and Stoyva (1969) to test whether feedback of ongoing EMG activity might be useful in facilitating deep muscle relaxation. Relaxation is a major therapeutic tool in and of itself, as well as being an important component of systematic desensitization (Wolpe 1958). Thus, the development of specific procedures to facilitate muscle relaxation is of considerable clinical import. Normal subjects were divided into three groups: one which received feedback of their frontalis EMG activity, a second which was provided feedback that was not related to their EMG activity, and finally, a group which received no feedback. The results after four training sessions indicated that the group which received correct feedback produced the greatest decreases in EMG, to approximately 50 percent of baseline values.

Subsequent to this pioneering work, Green, Walters, Green, and Murphy (1969) described the use and development of a technique for relaxation of single motor units recorded by surface electrodes and using a feedback meter. Their results were quite consistent with those reported earlier by Lindsley (1935), that subjects could very quickly learn to completely relax dorsal forearm muscles by using exteroceptive stimuli. Leaf and Gaarder (1971) later described methodological and technical concerns when attempting EMG biofeedback.

Budzynski and Stoyva (1973) performed a second analogue study with a different muscle group. In this study they assessed the ability of subjects to control masseter (jaw) muscle activity. Eighty subjects were divided into four groups that received the following experimental procedures: analogue feedback in which a tone varied in frequency in relationship to the EMG activity; a binary visual feedback in which a light indicated presence of EMG activity above a criterion level; an irrelevant feedback control group, and a no-feedback control group. Results for one training session indicated both accurate feedback procedures to be equally superior to both control procedures.

As the Budzynski and Stoyva (1973) study indicated, and as we noted in Chapter 2, there are several ways to present feedback to subjects. While these procedures are all termed biofeedback they may produce different effects. One simple technique of feedback, used successfully for controlling blood pressure by Elder *et al.* (1973) and Blanchard *et al.* (1975) is to provide discrete feedback at the end of each trial. This technique was contrasted with the more typical continuous feedback techniques for EMG control by Kinsman, O'Banion, Robinson, and Staudenmayer (1975). The discrete trials procedure involved providing verbal feedback approximately every two minutes as to whether the subject was reducing frontalis EMG levels. Results demonstrated a superiority during feedback and feedback maintenance periods for continuous feedback, with discrete feedback being superior to a no-feedback control. During a no-feedback condition to assess self-control, continuous feedback was superior to both discrete feedback and the no-feedback control, which were equal.

Rubow and Smith (1971) analyzed the effects of two types of continuous analogue feedback available from the average integrator display; moving average and intermittent average integration. Both procedures provide estimates of ongoing EMG activity for a limited number of intervals in which the raw EMG activity is sampled. In the moving average technique an average EMG level is obtained for the sample intervals in each interval, and as each sample is produced a new interval is added to the sample, while the old interval is dropped. Thus, a relatively continuous estimate of EMG activity is available. In the intermittent average technique the average of the set of samples is calculated, and a new sample is then begun.

Relatively discontinuous feedback is thus available. The moving average display is a smooth line, while the intermittent display is a choppy line.

Each of the 12 subjects was exposed to the moving average and intermittent average conditions, with feedback delays of 0.25 and 0.75 seconds for each type of feedback. The subjects' task was to match the feedback produced by biceps muscle activity on an oscilloscope to a moving target spot or the oscilloscope generated by a computer. Results clearly showed fewer errors when the moving average signal was available, and the optimal feedback display time was 0.75 sec.

Alexander, French, and Goodman (1975) also assessed two techniques for presentating feedback, visual versus auditory. While Budzynski and Stoyva (1973) had groups differing in this dimension, the conditions were confounded because the visual feedback was presented on a binary basis, while the auditory feedback was an analogue signal. Alexander *et al.* (1975) compared visual and auditory feedback of frontalis EMG, both of the analogue type. The results of the group study showed that only the subjects receiving auditory feedback with eyes closed showed a decrease in EMG level as compared with other groups with auditory feedback/eyes open, visual feedback, or no-feedback/eyes closed, which did not differ and showed no decrease in EMG level. As part of a larger study, Schandler and Grings (1976) evaluated analogue visual and tactile feedback in controlling frontalis EMG and found tactile feedback to be superior. In a second study, tactile feedback was compared with auditory, with no EMG differences observed between tactile and auditory feedback.

In addition to work on the optimum feedback mode, several researchers have made comparisons between biofeedback techniques and other forms of relaxation training for reducing muscle tension (Coursey 1975; Haynes, Moseley, and McGowan 1975; Reinking and Kohl 1975; Schandler and Grings 1976). Coursey (1975) compared the effects of continuous auditory feedback of frontalis EMG *with* instructions to relax and a cognitive technique for relaxation over a baseline and seven practice sessions. Results indicated biofeedback to be the superior technique for reducing EMG; however, subjective measures of anxiety decreased for all groups, independent of the treatment. Haynes *et al.* (1975) compared continuous auditory biofeedback with active relaxation, passive relaxation, a false feedback control condition, and a no-treatment control condition. Results again indicated biofeedback was the best technique, with passive relaxation next best while the other procedures were equal.

Three types of EMG feedback were compared with a progressive relaxation and a control group across three baseline and 12 treatment sessions by Reinking and Kohl (1975). The feedback conditions were standard EMG analogue biofeedback, EMG feedback plus a monetary reward for decreases in EMG activity, and EMG feedback plus progressive relaxation condition. Results showed all three feedback procedures to be about equal in reducing EMG activity, and superior to the relaxation and control procedures. The relaxation procedure did produce greater EMG reduction than was achieved by the subjects in the control group, who did not change over time. Self-reports of relaxation decreased across time for all subjects, independent of the group. Schandler and Grings (1976) found progressive relaxation equivalent to tactile EMG feedback for reducing both EMG activity and self-report of anxiety; moreover, both conditions of which were superior to a control group and a visual feedback group.

The reliable finding that biofeedback for EMG reduction is superior to relaxation training suggests that biofeedback techniques may be used instead of relaxation, or to supplant relaxation procedures. The data collected by Coursey (1975), Haynes *et al.* (1975), and Reinking and Kohl (1975) confirm this suggestion only partially, however, because these experimenters monitored only one muscle group, the frontalis. An adequate assessment of relaxation should be dependent upon reduction in muscle activity in various sites in the body. Alexander (1975) designed a study to test the utility of biofeedback to induce general body relaxation by providing continuous auditory EMG feedback for the frontalis muscle while simultaneously measuring EMG in arm and leg muscles. A control group received no feedback, but were instructed to relax. Results over the measurement days showed decrease in frontalis EMG over time for the feedback group, with no change for the control subjects. No decrease in activity of the other muscle groups was observed; in fact, increases in forearm EMG were apparent. In addition, subjective reports of relaxation were obtained during each session, and these did not correlate highly with actual EMG levels. Schandler and Grings (1976), however, reported significant reduction in frontalis EMG for subjects receiving progressive relaxation or tactile feedback of EMG activity while subjects receiving auditory feedback for frontalis activity showed both a reduction in frontalis EMG and decreased arm EMG activity over time. Differential changes in self-report correlated with EMG decreases with reduction in tension reported by relaxation and tactile feedback subjects.

Summary

The analogue studies presented indicate certain findings that are important to the appropriate clinical use of biofeedback. First, the studies consistently support the effects of feedback on EMG reduction, which cannot be accounted for by irrelevant feedback, sitting in a chair, or relaxing. Second, the results indicate biofeedback produces greater reduction in EMG in the muscle group for which feedback is given than another common treatment procedure for EMG reduction, relaxation. Third, the studies show that there is no reason to expect EMG control for one muscle to reliably produce changes in any other muscle group, since one study showed the positive side effect, while a second did not. Fourth, the studies that related EMG to self-report of tension and relaxation typically find no relationship between subjective and physiological measures of anxiety, with the exception of Schandler and Grings (1976). While lack of this relationship has been somewhat surprising, it is consistent with a large body of evidence (Hersen 1973; Lang 1968) indicating that the cognitive, physiological, and motoric response systems are relatively independent, such that changes in one system may not affect the second system. This independence will be discussed again when the use of EMG feedback for tension headaches and anxiety is presented.

Clinical Research

On the whole, the clinical uses of EMG biofeedback have fared well. The disorders in which biofeedback for muscle control has been used have been divided into two categories (Blanchard and Epstein 1977): those in which muscle activity is the major target response, and those in which muscle regulation is a technique to produce changes in another response mode. Most of the problems in the first category involve dysfunctional muscles, their dysfunctions arising as a result of disease or trauma to the body. The techniques used in treating these disorders are often called muscle reeducation procedures. Changes in a paralyzed muscle of a stroke patient is one example. The general type of problem in the second category includes problems in which the muscle, though not damaged, is not being regulated appropriately. It is assumed that changes in the regulation of the target muscle can affect some problem behavior, as headaches, or stuttering.

Muscle Reeducation

Within this category are two general types of problems. One involves increasing the activity in a dormant muscle, as when working with some paralyzed stroke patients. A second type is the reduction in muscle activity of overactive, or spastic, muscles, which may be important in torticollis or dystonia.

Increasing muscle activity

Marinacci and Horande (1960) presented the initial report of the use of the EMG feedback in muscle reeducation. The authors used auditory feedback, similar to that used by Basmajian in his basic research, to treat several different types of disorders. Clinical data are presented on patients with hemiplegia, reversible physiological block due to edema, muscle atrophy secondary to causalgia, muscle control after nerve injury, substitution of normal muscle control for paralyzed ones, and finally, control of paralysis in Bell's palsy and polio. Although the cases were not reported with appropriate controls, the anecdotal changes reported were impressive. They have thus been the basis for much of the subsequent work in the many areas of muscle reeducation.

Andrews (1963) presented data on improvement in upper extremity muscle functioning in 17 of 20 hemiplegics after only five minutes of training. Another report of EMG biofeedback to improve upper extremity muscle performance in hemiplegics was by Brudny, Korein, Levidow, Grynbaum, Lieberman, and Friedmann (1974). The authors indicate some recovery in 11 of the 13 cases, with maximal improvement noted in four of the 13 patients. Brudny, Korein, Grynbaum, Friedmann, Weinstein, Sachs-Frankel, and Belandres (1976) reported on the clinical changes in 45 hemiparetics after 8–12 weeks of audiovisual feedback therapy. Thirty-nine cases were treated for upper-extremity paralysis, with marked improvement in the functional use of the limb in 27 cases, and long-term improvement observed for 20 of these patients. Six others were provided training for lower extremity changes, with some changes for control during ambulation for three subjects.

A detailed analysis of the role of EMG biofeedback in upper extremity muscle retraining for two hemiplegics was recently conducted by Epstein, Malone, and Cunningham (1976). In the first case a baseline of voluntary muscle activity of the extensor digitorium muscle (responsible for finger extension) was collected, and then feedback was provided until noticeable improvement in EMG activity was observed. At this time feedback was withdrawn for one session, reinstituted for several sessions, withdrawn for another session, and finally provided again. Inspection of the data in Fig. 3.1 shows gradual improvement until feedback was withdrawn, at which time control decreased. The pattern of increase

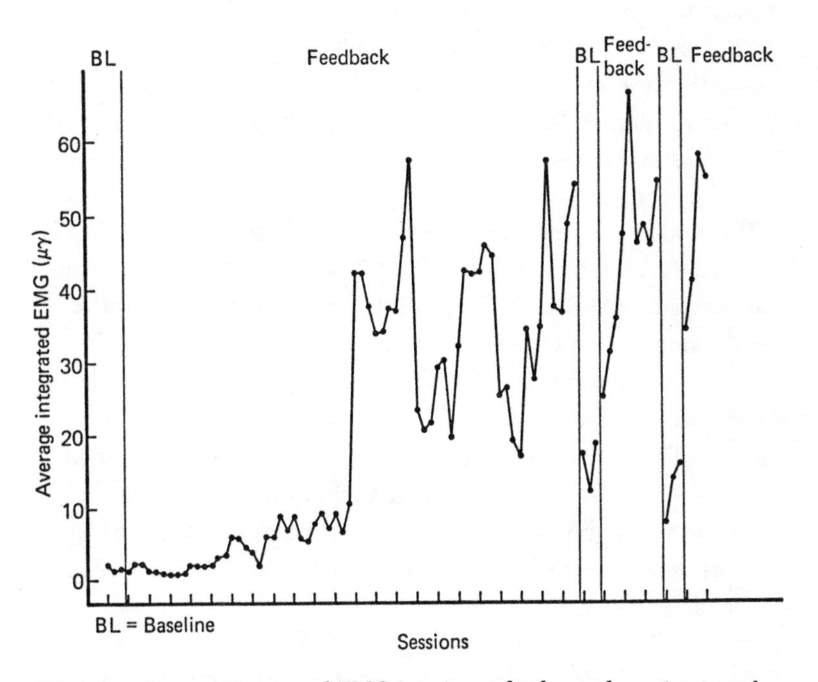

Fig. 3.1. Average integrated EMG in microvolts for each session as a function of experimental condition.

and decrease was replicated in the next two phases, demonstrating the role of feedback in increasing muscle activity.

The second case was an analysis detailing the process of change in biceps activity in an elderly poststroke patient. After demonstrating the reliable effect of feedback on increasing muscle function, control procedures were used to isolate the specific effect of feedback on the biceps muscle by ruling out any observed changes as a function of activity in the opposite biceps or the adjacent triceps. The feedback used to increase biceps activity in the target muscle was a light which was provided whenever EMG exceeded a criterion activity level. The procedures used to rule out observed changes in the target response as a function of these other muscles consisted of providing a light when a minimal EMG criterion was reached in the opposite biceps or same arm triceps and requiring the subject to turn on the light associated with the target biceps without turning on the light indicating activity in the other muscles. The data showed the subject was able to do this, indicating the observed biceps control was relatively specific to the target muscle.

The modification of lower extremity muscle retraining has been reported by Johnson and Garton (1973) and Basmajian, Kukulka, Naragan, and Tahebe (1975). Both studies were for foot drop, a condition involving the tibialis anterior muscle, which controls dorsiflexion. Johnson and Garton (1973) reported on changes in dorsiflexion, or the pivoting of the foot at the ankle, by using visual and auditory feedback from a diagnostic EMG machine in the laboratory, and then visual and auditory feedback from a portable machine to be used at home. Positive change was noted for all patients, with functional improvement of foot dorsiflexion for seven of the ten patients.

A controlled group study on muscle retraining was done by Basmajian *et al.* (1975) who compared standard physical rehabilitation procedures with physical rehabilitation plus biofeedback in two groups of ten patients each. The training involved both auditory and visual feedback. Results showed improvement for all patients, with the changes for the subjects receiving biofeedback being approximately twice as great as that for standard physical training. Follow-up measurement was conducted from four to 16 weeks post-treatment, with no decreases in muscle functioning over time.

Teng, McNeal, Krajl, and Waters (1976) attempted to compare the effects of nerve stimulation and biofeedback on foot dorsiflexion. Nerve stimulation is a procedure in which paretic muscles are contracted by the application of electrical current from an external power source to the nerve controlling the target muscle. Each of four subjects participated in three conditions designed to affect dorsiflexion: electrical stimulation, biofeedback, and electrical stimulation plus biofeedback. Functional movement in terms of torque generated by ankle dorsiflexion was assessed before and at three times after each of the three training periods. Results showed clear improvement for only one of the four subjects, with greater effects for this subject observed as a function of feedback than nerve stimulation.

Another example of muscle reeducation was presented by Booker, Rubow, and Coleman (1969) in a woman without voluntary control of left facial muscles following nerve damage in an automobile accident. Surgery was performed to activate facial nerves by trapezius (back and shoulder) and sternomastoid muscle movement; however functional control was not produced by this procedure. Thus, it was decided to teach the subject to make observable responses by manipulating new nerve/muscle connections. Feedback of the right and left facial muscles was provided on an oscilloscope, and the subject's first task was to match left facial activity to signals generated by a computer. She was then trained to match left facial signals with EMG activity produced by right facial muscles. This step was necessary to ensure symmetry of facial muscle control. The immediate effects of training were positive, with notable changes in her appearance during facial movements. A slight regression at four month follow-up was reversed by booster training sessions.

Decreasing muscle activity

There are numerous disorders that involve excessive muscle activity, with decreases in activity being the goal of treatment. Several studies have reported on the modification of the excessive head jerking present in torticollis, which is associated with a hypertrophied muscle on one side of the neck, and atrophied muscle on the other side. Brudny, Grynbaum, and Korein (1974) used an auditory and visual feedback procedure to produce equivalent amounts of muscle activity from sternocleidomastoid muscles on both sides of the neck when the head was kept in a neutral position. The laboratory EMG showed control by all patients for at least a 30-minute period, and six of the nine patients for periods of several hours. Brudny, Korein, Levidow, Grynbaum, and Friedmann (1974a) replicated these results with four more patients: control was shown in three of the four patients for 30 minutes and two of the four for periods of hours. Brudny *et al.* (1976) recently reported on important clinical changes in 26 of 48 spasmodic torticollis patients, with long-term (three month to three years) improvement in 19 of these patients.

Cleeland (1973) used auditory and visual feedback plus shock contingent on increases in muscle activity for ten torticollis patients. Eight patients showed control during feedback, and six were able to maintain control after feedback was withdrawn. Cleeland's data suggest that feedback plus contingent shock was superior to feedback alone.

The effects of visual feedback on relaxation of the spastic trapezius neck muscle in patients with neck injuries was reported by Jacobs and Felton (1969). The final results indicated the patients could demonstrate feedback influenced control comparable to feedback control in normal subjects.

Amato, Hermsmeyer, and Kleinman (1973) report the relaxation of the gastrocnemius muscle (the large muscle of the lower leg or calf) to facilitate foot dorsiflexion by use of a portable EMG unit for home use. After a two-month period the authors noted change in dorsiflexion and improvement in the subject's gait. Another attempt to inhibit antagonistic leg muscle activity to improve leg movement was by Swann, Wieringen, and Fokkema (1974). The authors attempted to decrease contraction of the peroneus longus muscle during quadriceps (thigh muscle) contraction in knee extension in seven subjects. The patients were seen for six sessions, each session including knee extension during physical therapy treatment and also during biofeedback. Results indicated significantly better control as a function of biofeedback with the biofeedback superior for five of the seven subjects.

One further use of EMG feedback to reduce undesired muscle activity was reported by Netsell and Cleeland (1973). They attempted to teach a 64-year-old Parkinsonian patient to control facial muscles in the lip, eye, and forehead to improve her speech and appearance. The authors reported considerable control of lip retraction following five sessions of analogue auditory EMG feedback.

Summary

The results of muscle reeducation studies are very impressive. Both increasing muscle strength and decreasing spasticity have been demonstrated in numerous laboratories with several target problems. Also, Booker *et al.* (1973) was able to train a subject to regulate muscle activity after a surgical procedure that provided new nerve-muscle connections. However, much additional research is necessary to clarify the relationship between muscle change and feedback training, and to indicate the number of important factors of treatment. Finally, the number of well-controlled investigations is very small.

Muscle Regulation

The goal of muscle retraining is to change muscle functioning in order to produce changes in functional movement. The muscle change is the target, with the EMG serving as a measure of muscle activity. In other disorders, the EMG is not the target problem response, but rather assumed is to be a mediator of the problem. In these disorders the muscles are not damaged, instead they are poorly *regulated* or hyperresponsive to environmental stimuli. Four different disorders will be discussed in this section: (1) modifying speech muscle activity to change silent reading; (2) changing muscle activity during speech to reduce stuttering; (3) decreasing forehead and neck muscle activity to reduce tension headache pain; and (4) reducing general muscle activity to decrease anxiety.

It is important to recognize in these disorders that changes in muscle activity is simply a means to the end of producing clinical change in a nonphysiological, or another physiological, response system. For example, assume a person has tension headaches (which may involve forehead muscle tension), reports of pain, and frequent absences from work. It is expected that decreasing the forehead tension will result in absence of pain and no interference with work behavior. However, changes in the muscle activity without collateral changes in pain would not represent a significant clinical effect.

Subvocalization

The studies in this section were designed to improve reading speed by decreasing "subvocal speech." The idea behind these treatment attempts is that slow readers may be making facial movements associated with speech and oral reading during silent reading, which may be responsible for a reduction in silent reading rates for these subjects. For this reason, Hardyck, Petrinovich, and Ellsworth (1966) attempted to reduce EMG activity from the laryngeal muscles by providing auditory feedback when the EMG activity exceeded a present criterion. The authors indicated reliable control of EMG activity during silent reading for the 17 college students tested. They then replicated (Hardyck and Petrinovich 1969) their procedures on college and high school subvocalizers. A control group of college students which received no feedback was used to assess the importance of feedback in EMG control. For the high school students there were differential effects of the feedback training on EMG levels with positive change found only for the average or above average IQ subjects. College students receiving feedback responded uniformly well, while no change was observed for any subjects not receiving feedback. However, the effects on reading speed were minimal and independent of the control of EMG activity. The major clinical effect was a reduction in the fatigue associated with long periods of reading.

McGuigan (1967) reported decreases in chin EMG during silent reading, when feedback was provided; however, he indicated similar changes were observed for control subjects not receiving feedback. While McGuigan used this data to question the importance of feedback in producing muscle control, it must be kept in mind that Hardyck *et al.* (1966, 1969) and McGuigan (1967) measured EMG activity from different muscles of the vocal apparatus. Finally in a very complex study, Aarons (1971) also indicated effects of EMG feedback on subvocal speech, but was not able to demonstrate any effects on mathematical problem solving, his somewhat unusual dependent measure of reading quality.

In summary, these results demonstrate that subvocal speech, as defined by throat EMG, can be reduced during silent reading. This does not have any apparent effect on reading rate, which decreases any clinical potential. A problem in this area is that the subvocalization was arbitrarily defined by various EMG measures, but no data were presented on the functional relationship between the EMG and reading behaviors. Clearly, the basic relationship between EMG and reading rate must be established before reductions in EMG could be expected to produce changes in the reading rate.

Stuttering

The use of EMG feedback for stuttering is very recent, with one study reported in 1975 (Guitar) and a second in 1976 (Lanyon, Barrington, and Newman). The basis for the use of EMG biofeedback in stuttering are reports by Williams (1975) demonstrating greater EMG activity in stutterers than nonstutterers, and differences in EMG activity preceding stuttered than nonstuttered words for stutterers (Shrum 1969). The implication of both these studies is that control of the EMG at various muscles sites in the speech apparatus would be sufficient to decrease stuttering.

Guitar (1975) provided a very detailed analysis of the relationship between EMG activity and stuttering. In an initial study Guitar measured EMG from three vocal sites, the chin, lip, and larynx, and one control site, the forehead. The training procedure involved teaching the subject to reduce the muscle activity in these sites, and then to implement this skill during reading of sentences. The particular skill to be learned was to relax the muscle just before speaking. Guitar identified three phonemes that were difficult for each of three subjects to pronounce, and then implemented the training using auditory feedback across the problem phoneme classes. His data indicated no changes during the forehead muscle control phases for any of the phoneme classes: when control was demonstrated for other muscle sites, there was an associated decrease in stuttered words. In a second study he implemented muscle control techniques in the clinical treatment of a stutterer. The target muscle was the chin. The results of the five-day treatment were very impressive, with virtual elimination of dysfluencies during both laboratory conversation and a recorded phone call up to nine months after treatment. Guitar indicates this subject was not a severe stutterer, and justifiably cautioned readers not to generalize on the basis of one case.

Lanyon *et al.* (1976) used visual feedback to decrease masseter (jaw) muscle activity in six stutterers over 10 to 18 one-hour sessions. The experimenters evaluated the importance of visual *meter* feedback in facilitating control by alternating feedback and no-feedback phases during word reading. The results indicated significant reduction in stuttering during the feedback phases. There was also some reported reduction over time during the nonfeedback phases, indicating some self-control when feedback was not available. The authors also report pilot work done on two stutterers with an earlier, somewhat inferior feedback system based on having the subjects observe an oscilloscope during reading, which also was associated with large-scale reductions of stuttering frequency.

Summary

The research in this area is fairly promising. Two studies have been completed, both of which used adequate controls, and both demonstrated important changes in speech dysfluencies. While the less controlled, anecdotal, clinical reports associated with most of the other areas of EMG biofeedback are certain to surface, the application of EMG control in stuttering appears to have a solid empirical base and may become an important clinical technique.

Muscle Contraction Headaches

In the previous uses of biofeedback to produce clinical effects the target problems were relatively clear-cut and easily measured. However, in the next two sections we discuss the use of muscle control for psychiatric problems that do not have such easily measurable referents, tension headaches and anxiety.

Tension, or muscle contraction, headaches are primarily a pain problem, with the patient reporting pain and having the headaches interfere with ongoing activities. It has been previously demonstrated that headache patients demonstrate greater levels of muscle tension than control patients (Malmo and Shagass 1949), and pain reports in muscle contraction disorders are produced during stimulus situations that elicit substantial muscle contractions (Malmo, Shagass, and Davis 1950). However, the specific relationship between headache pain and EMG activity has not been carefully studied, and headaches and EMG activity are not necessarily functionally related (Epstein and Abel 1977; Haynes, Griffin, Mooney, and Parise 1975). The researchers in this area have typically assumed that reports of headache pain are always a sign of increased muscle tension, and a reduction in muscle tension will thus be a sufficient treatment. However, with few exceptions (Budzynski, Stoyva, and Adler 1970; Epstein and Abel 1977) the experimenters have not assessed the subjects to ensure they do have a substantial amount of forehead muscle activity during or preceding headaches.

The first clinical report of EMG biofeedback in the treatment of headaches was by Budzynski, Stoyva, and Adler in 1971. In this report, auditory feedback training in the laboratory plus home relaxation was found to be related to decreases in laboratory EMG and extralaboratory headaches. These researchers (Budzynski, Stoyva, Adler, and Mullaney 1973) then conducted a controlled group outcome evaluation of biofeedback training. They randomly assigned 18 muscular contraction headache patients to three groups, a biofeedback plus relaxation training group, an irrelevant feedback plus relaxation training, and a no-feedback, no-relaxation control. Results indicated effects of feedback on laboratory EMG, and elimination of headaches in four to six subjects in the biofeedback group, with only one subject in the irrelevant feedback group and no control subjects showing a decrease. The authors report that the two subjects who were not headache-free did not consistently practice home relaxation, while the one patient in the irrelevant feedback group who improved did practice his relaxation regularly. While the patients were not specifically instructed in how to relax, the importance of home relaxation was emphasized by the authors, and has been shown to be a sufficient treatment by itself (Epstein, Webster, and Abel 1976; Tasto and Hinkle 1973).

Wickramasekera (1973) also demonstrated EMG feedback and relaxation training could be used to reduce the frequency and intensity of headache reports for five subjects. His procedures were not sufficient to identify whether relaxation training, biofeedback, or the combination of the two was responsible for the observed effects.

A detailed evaluation of the relationship between biofeedback and headache reports was assessed in a single-case study of a chronic muscular contraction headache patient by Epstein, Hersen, and Hemphill (1974). The authors evaluated the effects of music contingent on EMG decreases in both inpatient and outpatient phases. An A-B-A-B withdrawal design was used during the inpatient phase, with decreases in headaches and EMG activity. After the patient was discharged from the hospital, the headaches returned, but were suppressed by outpatient booster sessions. During the boosters an instructional control phase was used, which indicated the subject had no self-control over EMG decreases, but rather these effects were solely a function of the feedback. Headaches returned after treatment was stopped in the outpatient phase, and the subject was then trained in breathing exercises and exercises designed to loosen tight neck muscles. These were associated with almost total remission of headaches over the seven-month follow-up.

Epstein and Abel (1977) attempted a careful evaluation of the self-control of EMG activity as a function of biofeedback. Six chronic muscular contraction headache patients were provided 16 training sessions, each of which included baseline, contingent feedback, and self-control phases. No instructions to relax at home were provided. The laboratory results showed reliable feedback influenced EMG control, but no sustained self-control was observed. Also, no relationship was observed between EMG activity and headache reports in the laboratory. Clinical results, in terms of reduction in extralaboratory headaches, were positive for three subjects, with maintenance of effects for up to an 18-month follow-up. The three clinical successes were also the subjects with the *lowest* initial EMG activity.

Biofeedback techniques have been compared with relaxation procedures in three studies (Cox, Freundlich, and Meyer 1975; Haynes *et al.* 1975). This comparison is important for several reasons. First, since some of the most powerful results of biofeedback were obtained with instructions for home relaxation (Budzynski *et al.* 1973), it is important to evaluate the specific effects of relaxation alone. Secondly, if the procedures are equal, or even approximately equal, the reduced equipment requirements and technical assistance necessary for relaxation training would certainly favor relaxation on a cost–benefit basis. Cox *et al.* (1975) compared EMG auditory feedback plus relaxation training to relaxation alone and to a medication placebo. Data were collected during a two-week baseline, four weeks of treatment and four months of follow-up. Laboratory data indicated equal EMG changes as a function of either biofeedback or relaxation, both of which were superior to the placebo condition. As you may recall, these data are at odds with the analogue research showing biofeedback to be reliably superior to relaxation in reducing EMG activity (Reinking and Kohl 1975; Haynes *et al.* 1975). However, the interesting result is that both treatments were equally effective for self-report of headache activity and both of these were superior to the control group. Also, these positive effects were maintained at four-month follow-up.

Haynes *et al.* (1975) compared frontalis EMG biofeedback and relaxation training with a no-treatment control group. Self-report of headaches was assessed for a two-week baseline, during the three weeks of treatment, and at one week and five- to seven-month follow-up. Results were similar to those reported by Cox *et al.* (1975), with both treatment conditions being equally effective in reducing self-report of headaches. Chesney and Shelton (1976) compared headache frequency, duration, and severity for subjects exposed to muscle relaxation procedures, audiovisual analogue biofeedback, relaxation plus biofeedback, and a no-treatment control. Data collected over one week of baseline and two weeks of treatment indicate relaxation and biofeedback plus relaxation were superior to the biofeedback and control conditions. While effects of biofeedback alone were not significantly different from effects in the control condition, a reduction in headaches during biofeedback was observed, while no changes were observed within the control group.

Summary

The results of numerous studies indicate that biofeedback plus relaxation training can be useful in the treatment of muscular contraction headaches. However, recent research has questioned the role that biofeedback plays in the treatment. The first point is whether typical biofeedback procedures actually do produce self-control over muscle activity, which is a requirement for treatment success as biofeedback is currently conceptualized. A second point is whether biofeedback adds anything to the relatively inexpensive and easily implemented relaxation procedures. While biofeedback is consistently superior to relaxation in reducing frontalis EMG in nonclinical studies (Reinking and Kohl 1975; Haynes *et al.* 1975), this effect was not replicated in a clinical population (Cox *et al.* 1975) for whom relaxation training was shown to be equal to biofeedback in both EMG and headache lowering effects.

This area certainly requires more research, particularly to determine the relationship between EMG activity and headaches, since a self-report of headache pain in not necessary directly related to sustained muscle contractions. Consider the woman who reports headaches conveniently upon bedding down each evening with her not-so-beloved husband. In addition, it will be important to develop screening procedures to ensure the subject populations being treated are true muscular contraction headache patients. This requires selection of subjects on the basis of headache reports and evaluated muscle tension levels, a requirement met in very few studies (Budzynski *et al.* 1973; Epstein and Abel 1977). It is important to note these selections criteria were not followed in the investigations of Cox *et al.* (1975), Haynes *et al.* (1975) and Chesney and Shelton (1976) reporting equivalent control of muscular contraction headaches by relaxation training and biofeedback training.

Anxiety

It is often assumed that reports of anxiety are associated with increases in muscle tension. Treatments designed to reduce this tension, such as relaxation training, may then be useful in the management of anxiety. Biofeedback techniques also appear well suited to this task, as they are designed to lower muscle activity directly; moreover, they would also in the process provide objective measurement of EMG which could be useful in quantifying tension.

Raskin, Johnston, and Rondestvedt (1973) provided frontalis EMG feedback for ten chronically anxious patients who had previously been treated by minor tranquilizers and/or psychotherapy. The patients had anxiety symptoms, headaches, and insomnia. Subjects were asked to practice relaxation at home during treatment after they began to demonstrate EMG control. In general, positive results in terms of specific symptom reduction were found only for the headache and insomnia symptoms. There was little or no change in the more global self-report of anxiety.

In controlled studies Townsend, House, and Addario (1975) and Canter, Kondo, and Knotts (1975) had better success with frontalis EMG biofeedback for anxiety. Townsend *et al.* (1975) compared biofeedback with group therapy in two groups of fifteen patients over a two-week period. Results indicated that EMG and anxiety ratings from an adjective checklist decreased more for the feedback assisted relaxation subjects than for subjects in the control group. Canter *et al.* (1975) compared progressive relaxation and EMG feedback on EMG activity and global patient and therapist ratings of anxiety symptoms. The laboratory results indicated both procedures reduced frontalis EMG activity, but the biofeedback treatment produced greater decreases. The anxiety symptoms also decreased more for the patients receiving biofeedback than those who were trained in progressive relaxation, both in terms of patient and therapist ratings.

Summary

The results of studies to evaluate biofeedback to reduce anxiety seem to have produced somewhat equivocal results but the importance of the controlled studies (Townsend *et al.* 1975; Canter *et al.* 1975) far outweigh the single group outcome study (Raskin *et al.* 1973). There are two points to be considered by researchers in this area. The first is whether change in frontalis EMG is equivalent to complete bodily relaxation. This question is raised because of the relative independence of muscle groups; changing frontalis activity may have no effect on other muscle groups (Alexander *et al.* 1973). In addition, it is unclear whether changes in EMG activity are a sufficient condition for changes in self-report of anxiety, since numerous studies have shown poor relationships between EMG changes and reports of tension (for example, Mathews and Gelder 1969; Reinking and Kohl 1975; Alexander 1975). According to Schachter

(1971), it can be assumed that reports of anxiety are related to both physiological and cognitive changes, such that changes in the physiological state of the organism is a *necessary*, but may not be a *sufficient*, condition to change reports of emotional experiences.

Summary

In this chapter selected studies on the clinical applications of EMG biofeedback were reviewed. The findings of research in this area are very positive, and are certainly among the most consistent in any area of biofeedback. Studies have consistently demonstrated regulation of muscle activity in various sites and even in damaged muscles. The clinical uses of EMG biofeedback are very numerous, and marked changes have been produced in very debilitating problems that are resistant to therapeutic efforts, including muscle paralysis, headaches and anxiety reports.

There is still much research to be performed to refine the use of EMG biofeedback. There are several very interesting questions that remain unanswered. They include, for example, studying how a paralyzed muscle can be trained to move when the continuity of brain to muscle interconnections has been interrupted. Is it possible, and maybe probable, that a different area of the brain is responsible for the recovery of function? Second, what is the precise relationship between EMG changes and reports of headache pain and anxiety? Can functional relationships be determined which firmly establish that EMG reductions will reduce headache reports or anxiety symptoms? And third, and possibly in the long run most important, can a technology of self-management be developed so that patients can be trained to control EMG activity in the absence of experimenter-provided feedback?

4

Electroencephalogram

Measurement and Meaning

In this chapter, rather than discussing the use of biofeedback with a particular organ system, we deviate somewhat and describe instead the biofeedback research with one particular measurement technique used with an organ system. The organ system is the central nervous system (CNS) made up of the brain and spinal cord, and the measurement technique is the electroencephalogram (EEG).

The existence of the EEG patterns was discovered in 1929 by Berger. They are usually measured by electrodes attached to the scalp or inserted just below the skin of the scalp. The recorded signals are typically of very low voltage, in the range of a few microvolts (one-millionth of a volt), and a fairly high frequency (1 to 50 cycles per second or hertz [Hz]).

For the most part the EEG represents the condition and state of the cerebral cortex, the most highly developed part of the brain and the site of intellectual functions. Its primary use has been by neurologists as a noninvasive diagnostic tool. Various disorders of the CNS can be detected through the EEG including (sometimes) the presence of tumors and of seizure disorders (epilepsy). Sleep researchers have also used the EEG to identify the various stages of sleep.

The cerebral cortex is, of course, made up of millions of neurons, all of which emit tiny electrical signals as they discharge. The EEG, however, does not represent the firing of any specific neurons; rather the EEG represents an averaged signal from many cells. At times there is relatively synchronous firing or discharge of thousands of cortical neurons which leads to the recording of somewhat regular patterns in the EEG.

The four prinicipal rhythms or patterns of EEG activity are defined (somewhat arbitrarily) by their frequency and usually have various mental states or degrees of arousal associated with them. These are listed in Table 4.1.

An example of the most frequently studied activity of the EEG, the alpha rhythm, is presented in Fig. 4.1. This represents a recording with monopolar electrodes between the left parietal region and

Table 4.1 Principal Rhythms or Activities of the Human EEG

Name	Frequency (Hz)	State usually associated
Alpha	8–13	Relaxed wakefulness, especially with eyes closed
Beta	14–30	Mentally alert and "thinking"
Theta	4–7	Early stages of sleep
Delta	1–3	Deeper sleep

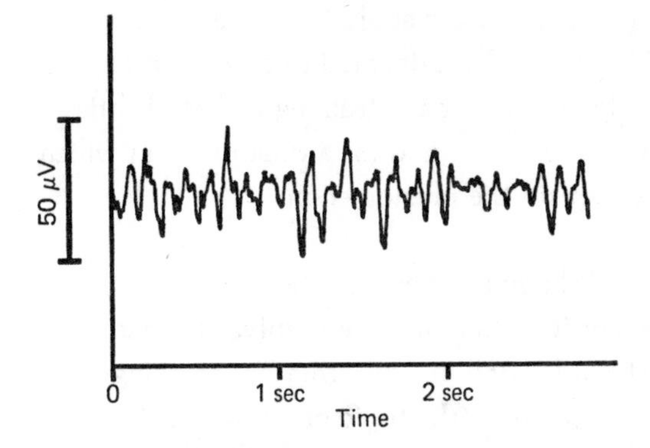

Fig. 4.1. Example of human EEG from left parietal region containing alpha rhythm.

the right ear. The predominant frequency of activity is 8.5 Hz with an average amplitude of about 30 microvolts (μV).

Basic Research

The basic research in biofeedback training for control of the EEG has followed a course of development much like that seen in the cardiovascular system, especially with heart rate. The particular response which has been most studied is the alpha rhythm and yet, until recently, few clinical applications of alpha biofeedback training had been reported. The reasons for this widespread interest in alpha biofeedback are similar to those which led to the amount of research on heart rate: (1) it was the first aspect of the EEG to be used in biofeedback studies; (2) it is relatively easy (among components of the EEG) to measure and give feedback of; and (3) the subjective reports of subjects in alpha training experiments aroused much interest.

Like the biofeedback research on control of heart rate, alpha biofeedback-training research has had several phases in its development: (1) an initial phase devoted both to the demonstration of the phenomenon and an exploration of the subjective experiences of research participants; (2) a later phase devoted to an exploration of parameters involved in alpha biofeedback training and to skeptics' attempts to dismiss the phenomenon; and (3) a final phase in which an attempt was made to explain the phenomenon.

Phase 1—demonstration of the phenomenon

In the 1960s, three different investigators, Joe Kamiya, Barbara Brown, and Joseph Hart, all located in California but working independently, reported research on the topic of autocontrol or feedback control of alpha activity by the use of the EEG.

Kamiya (1962) seems to have been the earliest worker in this field. In 1968 he described the results of several studies in a very influential article in *Psychology Today.* The basic paradigm used by Kamiya involved auditory feedback and discrimination training: a tone or bell was on when alpha was present and off when some other EEG activity was present. After some number of training trials, the subject's task was to be able to tell which kind of EEG signal the subject was producing. Kamiya reported that 80 to 90 percent of a large number of subjects learned to make the discrimination and were able to produce alpha or nonalpha activity in the EEG to a significant degree. In a second study, ten subjects were given feedback for shifting the dominant frequency of their alpha activity. Over a number of trials they were able to shift it significantly (by about 10–12 percent or about one Hz).

One of the most influential aspects of Kamiya's paper (1968) was the description of the subjective states reported by his subjects when they were in an "alpha state." These included "not thinking," "letting the mind wander" and "an alert calmness, a singleness of attention," "tranquil, calm, and alert." Allegedly about half of the subjects reported the alpha state to be very pleasant. The close resemblence of these self-reports to those given by practitioners of various kinds of meditation, especially Zen and yoga, and the reports of much alpha activity in the EEG of Zen masters, while their eyes were open, was probably the beginning of the idea that alpha biofeedback training might be a shortcut to achieving the benefits of meditation.

In a later investigation Nowlis and Kamiya (1970) ran 16 subjects in a single auditory feedback session with baseline, increase alpha, and decrease alpha conditions. Ten other subjects were run in the same conditions with eyes open. Afterwards subjects were interviewed as to strategies used to control the tone.

Results showed significant changes in percent of time during which alpha was present or absent during increase alpha and decrease alpha trials, respectively, for both the subjects run with eyes open and those run with eyes closed. The interviews yielded results very similar to those reported earlier by Kamiya (1968); that is, there were frequent reports of relaxation, letting go, and awareness of internal states during the alpha generation condition and reports of being alert, vigilant, and visually attentive in the alpha suppression condition.

Another of the original workers in this area, Hart (1967) studied the ability of subjects to increase alpha index (the percent of time during a trial for which significant alpha activity is present in the EEG) as a result of auditory feedback training with eyes closed. All three groups of subjects in Hart's study were run for 13 sessions spread over approximately 6–8 weeks. One group received eight sessions of auditory feedback and information on their performance at the end of each session; a second group received identical feedback training but no additional information, while the final group received no feedback but had their EEG monitored for 13 sessions.

Results showed that all eight subjects in the first condition showed significant increases in alpha index from beginning to end of training while six of eight subjects in the second (feedback training only) condition showed significant increases; three of five subjects in the monitoring-only condition also showed increases. The subjects receiving alpha feedback training plus the session-by-session feedback on performance showed statistically greater improvement than the other two groups.

Hart also interviewed his subjects and found that "only the subjects who achieved a doubling or tripling or greater increase of their alpha levels report much of a subjective change during the training sessions." Also the reports were varied but agreed that "a higher alpha level was pleasant and restful." A state of passive alertness seemed to sustain the alpha rhythm.

The third pioneer in alpha biofeedback training, Barbara Brown, has reported on the ability of subjects to increase alpha abundance (similar to Hart's [1967] alpha index) when feedback is given in a visual mode and subjects have their eyes open (1970, 1971). In addition to demonstrating that this form of feedback is effective in helping subjects increase the time during which their EEGs show alpha activity, Brown has been especially concerned with the subjective experiences of subjects who were showing relatively higher amounts of alpha (1970) and with the subjective experiences associated with alpha, beta, and theta activity in the EEG (1971). Her results show that subjects can learn to significantly increase alpha abundance (or percent time alpha) with visual feedback, both within a session and across sessions. Her subjects did seem to reach an asymptote by about the sixth training session, however (1970).

In the area of the subjective experience of the research participants, she found in the first study (1970) that a majority of subjects who showed good control of alpha, and relatively high percent time alpha, reported "losing all awareness except of light signal" or else "drifted or floated" and that most subjects had generally positive affective responses and felt relaxed.

In the second study (1971) she refined her techniques for eliciting subjective responses to the different EEG states while also teaching subjects to alternate between alpha, beta, and theta activity as the predominant EEG activity. The generalizations which appear in her report were that alpha activity tended to be associated with pleasant feelings, tranquility, and/or "increased awareness of thoughts and feelings, whereas beta was associated with either worry, anger, and fear of tension, alertness, and excitement." There were few consistencies in the reports on experiential aspects of theta but they seemed to cluster around memories of problems, problem solving, and planning.

Comment. By the end of the 1960s these conclusions seemed warranted by the mainstream of research in alpha biofeedback training: (1) it was possible for subjects to learn both to generate higher levels of alpha activity and to suppress alpha activity through the use of biofeedback training; (2) feedback could be given in either the auditory mode or visual mode with eyes either opened or closed and the acquisition phenomena still obtained; (3) it was possible to teach subjects to reliably generate or suppress alpha activity in the absence of feedback after biofeedback training, some few subjects seemed able to do this initially without biofeedback training. Furthermore, subjects could reliably discriminate when they were producing relatively greater amounts of alpha in their EEG.

Finally, the overwhelming consensus from the reports of subjects of their subjective experiences when showing relatively high percentages of alpha in their EEG (the so-called *alpha state)* was that the alpha state was pleasant, characterized by a passive alertness, and a "letting go of the mind." Investigators were especially interested in the subjective report data because the subjects' reports were very similar to those of persons engaging in various forms of meditation, especially Zen or yoga. Moreover, it had been reported that advanced practitioners of these forms of meditation showed high percentages of alpha in their EEG while meditating. People thus were drawn to the conclusion that alpha biofeedback training might be a shortcut, or electronic, way of achieving the benefits of meditation and that some or all of the benefits of meditation, especially yoga training, might be available to those who participated in alpha biofeedback training. In any event many speculations about "altered states of consciousness" and relations between subjective states and EEG patterns (Brown, 1971) began to appear and have not subsided.

Phase 2—skepticism

As with several other areas of biofeedback research the initial set of findings and truisms in alpha biofeedback training came under attack from later investigators who failed to replicate the initial results. Thus it was not long before new investigators began to challenge the generalizations listed at the end of Phase 1. In the interest of brevity, only the most important of these will be reviewed here.

Paskewitz and Orne (1973) took the position that there are two ways to demonstrate voluntary control of alpha density (a parameter similar to Hart and Brown's representing relative frequency of alpha activity's being present in the EEG): either (1) through comparing enhance or generate alpha trials with suppress alpha trials or (2) through comparing enhance or generate trials with the appropriate stable baseline. They argued from their data and that of others that the demonstrations in (1) were demonstrations only of the ability to suppress alpha which had long been known. They next presented data from two experiments which questioned whether alpha density ever goes above baseline values with biofeedback training, *if the optimal baseline conditions are used.* In both studies baseline levels of alpha density were determined both with eyes open and eyes closed. In one study the room was completely dark; it was dimly lit in the other. Training was carried on for a number of feedback trials, alternated with rest periods, for six sessions in one study and seven in the second.

The chief findings were (1) "subjects can acquire volitional control of alpha activity only under (environmental) conditions which normally lead to decreased densities," such as with eyes open in dimly lit room; (2) no alpha densities were observed in feedback training beyond an individual's initially demonstrated physiological range (or baseline levels with eyes closed and relaxed); (3) alpha feedback training may enable a subject to overcome suppressing effects when they were present. (4) Finally, they interpreted the subjective experiences reported (which were not nearly as uniformly positive) to be a consequence of the subjects' acquiring skills in disregarding stimuli in the external, and perhaps internal, environment which ordinarily inhibit alpha.

A second major investigation into the necessary and sufficient conditions for the "alpha experience" was reported by Walsh (1974). He sought to determine the interactive effects of a high alpha density produced through alpha biofeedback training and an "instructional set" either favorable or not favorable to having the "alpha experience" on subjective reports. Thus he performed a factorial experiment in which subjects received feedback training designed to enhance or suppress alpha activity crossed with an instructional set either consistent with an alpha experience or not consistent.

The results revealed that neither the high alpha state resulting from feedback training nor the positive instructional set alone was sufficient to lead to subjective reports consistent with the alpha experience, and, in fact, alone neither differed from the neutral set—low alpha condition. However, with the combination of high alpha state and positive expectancy subjects' reports were consistent with the alpha experience; thus both appear necessary but neither is sufficient.

Walsh's results particularly help clarify why people in normal (nonbiofeedback) physiologically produced high alpha state, eyes closed in dark room, (hence high alpha density) do not report the alpha experiences. It is as if subjects have to learn or be told how to interpret the subjective aspects of the high alpha state.

The oculomotor hypothesis

At about the same time an entirely different explanation of the alpha biofeedback training effects and the concomitant subjective experiences was being proposed by Mulholland and his associates, especially Erik Peper.

Mulholland had conducted a long series of experiments on cortical alpha activity, especially the effects of various visual parameters on blocking alpha activity recorded from the occipital region (the area of the cortex in the back of the head that is most intimately associated with vision). In the mid-1960s he turned to studying the effects of feedback on occipital alpha (summarized in Mulholland 1968, 1973). Thus his work was more concerned with the suppression of alpha activity than with generating it.

This work eventually led to a series of hypotheses or a model to account for the alpha biofeedback findings. Prior to Mulholland's work it had been thought that "attention" led to alpha blocking. This was restated in a elegant but simple form by Peper (1970) that subjects learn "to look" to suppress alpha activity and "to not look" to enhance it.

Mulholland eventually hypothesized that three oculomotor (having to do with the movements that control vision, primarily the muscles that move the eyeball) processes were involved in blocking occipital alpha: (1) convergence movements (when the two eyes turn inward in order to focus on something near the person); (2) lens accommodation (when the relative thickness or thinness of the lens of the eye is changed by the muscles which control it); and (3) pursuit-tracking movements of the eyes, that is, the eyes usually move in unison to tract a moving object.

Mulholland and Peper (1971) eventually concluded, based on several experiments, that "the general hypothesis . . . is that the combined processes of pursuit tracking, convergence, and lens accommodation will reliably block or markedly attenuate the alpha rhythm . . . auto regulation of the alpha rhythm by alpha feedback training is likely to be mediated by learned control of oculomotor and lens adjustment processes" (pp. 573–574).

Comment. With the work of Mulholland and Peper, there came into the mainstream of alpha biofeedback work a second viable explanation for most of the observed data in the field. One could conceptualize the field, as Plotkin did (1976), as being confronted with two opposing *views* of how subjects gained control of the alpha rhythm in biofeedback training: (1) *a cognitive* strategy which held that, with the aid of biofeedback training, subjects learned to develop a calm, relaxed, passive state of mind and attention which resulted in a high alpha state. (2) The second *strategy* was the *oculomotor* strategy of Mulholland which held that subjects learned to control various aspects of the oculomotor control system in biofeedback training and that appropriate tuning of this system led to the high alpha state.

Plotkin's Work

What was obviously needed was a resolution of these two competing theories through a direct comparison. This was done in an elegantly designed study by Plotkin (1976). Although space considerations do not permit a full description of his study, it will be briefly summarized below.

Plotkin (1976) ran five groups of subjects in a series of trials on which they were to enhance or suppress the alpha activity in their occipital EEG. Each block of trials included a resting period to serve as a baseline for the trial. Moreover, blocks of trials were run both in darkness and in dim light. All trials were conducted with eyes open. Instructions in how to control alpha, either a cognitive strategy, or oculomotor strategy, or no instructions were crossed with either feedback or no feedback, except the no-feedback, no-strategy group was omitted.

Plotkin was careful to instruct his subjects to refrain from using their specific strategy during the baseline periods. Also he used a very sensitive measure of alpha activity. Finally, subjects were interviewed extensively after the experiment to determine what strategies they had used and what they had experienced. The actual instructions for the oculomotor groups involved telling subjects to let their vision blur and not to focus their eyes.

The results of this study go far in clarifying the picture on alpha control and the alpha experience. The conclusions from this study, based on its results, are (1) "feedback-augmented enhancement and suppression of occipital alpha strength is always mediated by learned control of oculomotor processes, although sometimes persons are not aware that they are employing this strategy . . . ; (2) "feedback together with simple oculomotor instructions leads to more successful alpha control than either alone"; (3) high or enhanced levels of occipital alpha strength are not invariably accompanied by the "alpha experience," rather "if a person is not led to expect it, the alpha experience will usually not occur during occipital alpha enhancement feedback"; (4) alpha feedback per se is neither necessary for nor especially facilitative of the achievement of the alpha experience." (p. 66)

Comment. One other implication of Plotkin's (1976) results is that the beneficial effects of meditation, well documented by Benson (1975), probably come from the regular practice of meditating rather than from some physiological connection with a high alpha state. The high degree of alpha seen in the EEGs of advanced meditators are thus a result of the meditative experience and practice, not a cause of the experience. Instant meditation through alpha biofeedback training does not seem to be the way!

Clinical Applications

The vast bulk of clinical applications of EEG biofeedback training fall into two broad categories: (1) applications of alpha training; and (2) applications of sensorimotor rhythm training.

Alpha Training

The attempts at applying alpha biofeedback training to clinical problems have followed somewhat logically from the basic research on alpha training, particularly from the early reports on the subjective experiences of subjects in a high alpha state. More specifically, alpha biofeedback training has been used in the treatment of (1) pain, particularly chronic pain, (2) drug and alcohol abuse, (3) general psychiatric problems which were anxiety mediated, and (4) seizure disorders.

Alpha biofeedback and pain

The use of alpha biofeedback training in the treatment of pain follows somewhat logically from two observations: (1) there was fairly uniform agreement from the early alpha biofeedback research that the subjective reports of persons who learned to produce high levels of alpha in their EEGs were very similar to the reports of advanced practitioners of some of meditation and that many of the latter showed high levels of alpha activity in their EEGs while meditating; (2) there were reports (Anand, Chhina, and Singh 1961) in which some yoga meditators were able to endure what would ordinarily be very painful stimulation, without apparent discomfort while they were meditating. During meditation their EEGs showed high levels of alpha activity. Investigators then wondered if training patients with chronic intractable pain to produce a high alpha state would relieve the pain.

Gannon and Sternbach (1971) first tested this idea with a patient with frequent, very painful headaches. He received approximately 70 sessions of alpha biofeedback training and gradually learned to produce a fairly high alpha level in his EEG even with his eyes open. The clinical results were less impressive, however, in that the patient tended to feel better when he did not have a headache but he was unable to inhibit the pain through producing alpha when he did have a headache. Unfortunately no systematic data were presented on headaches or pain levels so that overall clinical benefit is difficult to assess.

Following similar reasoning, McKenzie, Ehrisman, Montgomery, and Barnes (1974) conducted a controlled group outcome study of the treatment of tension headaches with alpha biofeedback. The control group received relaxation training by tape recordings. After one week of baseline recording of headache frequency and duration, both groups were given five weeks of twice weekly sessions.

For some unspecified reason, no statistical comparisons were made between groups. The biofeedback group was reported to have an average reduction in hours of headache per week of 79.4 percent. No details of how this percent reduction was calculated nor whether it was statistically significant were given. Follow-up reports at one and two months showed that this reduction had held up (77.4 percent). The authors noted that the relaxation group also showed reduction in symptoms. However, they claimed the biofeedback group showed "earlier symptom reduction" and "earlier production of alpha." No systematic data were given about the relation of increase in alpha activity to change in headaches in the experimental subjects.

This study, while a controlled group outcome study, has two major faults: the lack of data analysis does not allow meaningful conclusions to be drawn; second, the biofeedback treatment was not significantly more effective than a relaxation procedure. Thus, there is little evidence for the specific efficacy of alpha biofeedback training.

The final study in this area is an ambitious attempt by Melzack and Perry (1975) to treat chronic, continuous, unremitting pain of known somatic pathological origin, which could not be completely blocked by analgesics or narcotics. Three conditions were used: (1) training with alpha biofeedback alone for eight sessions ($n=6$); (2) training in hypnosis with suggestions of pain relief, relaxation and increased self-control for four sessions, ($n=6$); (3) a combination of hypnotic training and alpha biofeedback training for a total of ten sessions ($n=12$). Results were assessed primarily with a self-report questionnaire of pain description (McGill Pain Questionnaire) which taps the multiple dimensions of pain. This was administered before and after every session.

Results showed that the group receiving the combination treatment showed significantly greater reductions in pain reports within the treatment sessions than within the initial baseline sessions. Neither of the other two groups showed comparable significant reductions. Moreover, 58 percent of the patients receiving the combination treatment reported at least a 33 percent reduction in pain. For those patients who did experience substantial reduction in pain in the session, there was also a generalization of the relief for one to four hours posttraining.

Unfortunately the design of this study and the method of data analysis seriously limit its interpretability and usefulness. First, the group receiving the combination treatment also received more treatment sessions; therefore it could be that the length of treatment alone is responsible for the results. Second, the use of unequal group sizes adds to the confusion. Finally, no comparisons were made *between* the three groups. It appears that the combination treatment did not lead to significantly more pain relief than either of the individual treatments.

All groups showed increases in EEG alpha with the group receiving the alpha biofeedback training alone showing the least increase in alpha. The authors conclude, on a basis which is not at all clear, that the alpha biofeedback training does play a part in the control of pain, but that an increase in alpha in the EEG is not a necessary part of the process.

Comment. At this point there has been no clear-cut demonstration of the utility of alpha biofeedback training for the control of pain. In every study for which even some has been shown, experimental design or data analysis problems preclude drawing any definite conclusions on efficacy. Given this state plus what we now know about the effects of alpha biofeedback training from Plotkin's (1976) work, it does not seem that alpha biofeedback training has much to offer over less equipment-oriented training such as in relaxation, meditation, or hypnosis.

Alpha biofeedback and drug or alcohol abuse

The use of alpha biofeedback training with alcohol and drug abusers is also based on the early accounts of the subjective reports of subjects in a high alpha state, or the so-called alpha experience. The description of this experience as an altered state of consciousness with many concomitant positive affective components is very similar to what many drug abusers describe as the subjective aspects of their "highs" or drug-altered mood. Thus the rationale for using alpha biofeedback training to treat alcohol and drug abusers is to see if they will learn to substitute the "high" or relaxation or calmness from the alpha experience for the high or relaxation from drugs or alcohol.

Kurtz (1974) reported on a program in which alpha biofeedback training was added to the treatment regimen of one group of alcohol and drug abusers while it was not added for a comparable group. The standard treatment regimen included group and individual therapy, vocational counseling, Alcoholics Anonymous as well as other group activities. The only posttreatment difference between the two groups reported was lower BP for the experimental group (average decrease 17.4 mm Hg systolic and 8.8 mm Hg diastolic) while that for the control group rose slightly. No statistical comparisons were made and no other differences were noted.

In a second study Lamontagne, Hand, Annable, and Gagnon (1975) reported on the treatment of 24 young drug abusers (all used marijuana regularly while some used hallucinogens; narcotic and amphetamine users were exluded). One group received four sessions of alpha biofeedback training; a second group received four sessions of EMG biofeedback training, while the third group received false feedback. All groups received four 40-minute treatment sessions.

Results showed no significant in-session increase in EEG alpha for the alpha biofeedback group but a significant reduction in frontalis EMG for the EMG feedback group. The false feedback group showed no change. Although there was a marked reduction in use of marijuana during training for all three groups (approximately 50 percent of patients reported abstaining from the drug), no statistically significant effects were found. Moreover, at follow-ups over a six-month period, a marked return to drug use by about half of those who stopped during treatment was noted. There was also a reduction in self-report of anxiety at the one month follow-up for all subjects combined but this did not hold up later.

In a third related study, Jones and Holmes (1976) studied the EEGs of alcoholics and the ability of this population to learn control of alpha through biofeedback training. The results showed a trend ($p = 0.07$) for nonalcoholics to have more alpha in their EEGs than alcoholics. Secondly, the alcoholics failed to show significant increases in EEG alpha with three sessions of alpha biofeedback training over that shown by alcoholics receiving false feedback.

Comment. The benefits of alpha biofeedback training for alcohol or drug abusers has not been demonstrated. It has been shown in these studies that special attention can lead to some reduction in substance abuse but that reduction does not seem attributable to alpha biofeedback training.

Alpha biofeedback and general psychiatric problems

The treatment of general psychiatric problems through alpha biofeedback training is based on the reported subjective experiences of subjects in a high alpha state, especially the reports of calmness, tranquility and relaxation. If psychiatric patients whose problems are primarily due to anxiety could learn to produce high levels of alpha and gain self-control of the resulting experience of tranquility and relaxation, it follows that the patients would be much improved.

Such was the reasoning of Glueck and Stroebel (1975) in their very ambitious research program on the clinical applications of alpha biofeedback training. Groups of psychiatric inpatients at a well-known private psychiatric hospital, The Institute of Living, were assigned to one of three conditions: relaxation training by autogenic training ($n=12$), alpha EEG biofeedback ($n=26$), and transcendental meditation (TM) ($n=187$).

Some interesting results were obtained. Patients in the relaxation training group all complained after two or three weeks that the procedure was boring and asked to stop. Twenty-six patients completed 15 sessions of alpha biofeedback training. Although they developed some ability to increase alpha density while receiving feedback, they had much difficulty in demonstrating any self-control. The authors (Glueck and Stroebel 1975, p. 307) state:

> For a number of patients in the alpha biofeedback group, the attempts to produce alpha resulted in an increase in tension and anxiety because of the uncertainty about the results and did little to promote the relaxation and tranquility that were the primary goals of the technique. We therefore terminated the alpha biofeedback phase of the project after 26 patients had been through this type of biofeedback training.

The subjects receiving TM did very well. Of 96 patients who completed more than eight weeks of training, 83 were discharged. Comparisons of these patients with non-TM-trained patients from the general population, matched for sex, age, and MMPI profile, revealed significantly greater improvement and discharge rates than the controls ($p<0.001$). In fact, patients trained in TM did better than the hospital population as a whole ($p<0.05$).

Although the diagnostic groupings of the patients were not given, and the method of evaluation of improvement is somewhat unclear, the global impression remains that TM training helped the patients' hospital course appreciably while alpha biofeedback training was ineffective at best and possibly detrimental. This is consistent with our earlier speculation that the beneficial effects of meditation come from the regular practice of meditation rather than through the achieving of any particular EEG state.

In another study in which alpha biofeedback training has been used to treat psychiatric patients, Mills and Solyom (1974) treated five patients with obsessive ruminations. In this instance the rationale was that a high alpha state was incompatible with ruminations and hence the biofeedback training might block the neurotic symptoms.

The two patients who showed the most evidence of "learning," that is, an increased percentage of time in the treatment session during which alpha was being emitted, discontinued treatment early. For the three who remained for the full 20 sessions, there was little evidence of increased alpha. Four of the five patients reported an absence of ruminations during their feedback-assisted alpha state while the fifth patient had a marked decrease in ruminations. Therefore, within treatment sessions, the patients were much improved. Unfortunately this did not generalize at all outside of the treatment sessions.

Comment. At this point alpha biofeedback training does not seem especially helpful in treating psychiatric patients. In fact, there has been no consistent clinical benefit in any of the problem areas summarized in this section. It seems that alpha biofeedback training is an interesting phenomenon which many normals experience as pleasant but which has little or no clinical utility. Where it has shown some utility, the beneficial effects are probably achievable in some other fashion and the beneficial effects do not seem related to achievement of a high alpha state.

Sensorimotor Rhythm Training and Epilepsy

Since it is well recognized that many patients with seizure disorders (epilepsy) also show abnormalities in their EEG, even in a nonseizure state, it was logical that some investigators would seek to use EEG biofeedback training to treat epilepsy. There have been two anecdotal case reports of the use of alpha biofeedback training to treat seizure disorders. Both cases (Johnson and Meyer 1974; Rouse, Peterson, and Shapiro 1974) involved various psychotherapeutic procedures other than biofeedback training but did nevertheless show some improvement.

The most promising work in the treatment of seizure disorders through biofeedback training has been that by Sterman and his associates (Sterman, 1973; Sterman, and Friar, 1972). Their procedure involves teaching epileptic patients to increase the occurrence of the so-called sensorimotor rhythm (SMR), a 12–14 Hz rhythm recorded over the sensorimotor cortex. (There is a portion of the cerebral cortex located roughly in a band across the top of the head between the ears which controls all voluntary motor activity, that is movement, and also serves as the reception area for all tactile sensory inputs; this band is called the sensorimotor cortex.)

In most people, both normal subjects and patients suffering from seizure disorders, there is very little of this activity normally present in the EEG. In the treatment regimen described by Sterman, the SMR activity is detected by a special EEG filter tuned to the 12–14 Hz band/pass and patients are given visual feedback when it is present. Gradually patients learn to produce more and more of this particular rhythm. Correspondingly, other EEG activity, particularly some high energy activity in lower frequencies tends to decrease. In this work, Sterman seems to be seeking relatively permanent changes in the EEG of the patient (Sterman 1973) rather than teaching them a self-control technique to use to abort seizures.

Detailed reports (Sterman 1973) have been presented on four cases: (1) a 7-year-old boy with a mixed seizure disorder: major motor seizures plus petit mal variant; (2) a 23-year-old woman with a focal major motor disorder; (3) an 18-year-old man with a mixed seizure disorder and petit mal variant; (4) a 46-year-old man with adult petit mal seizure. In all four cases there were both significant clinical improvement in terms of reduced seizure frequency and periods when the patient was seizure-free, and significant changes in both the clinical EEG in terms of decreases in abnormal (i.e., spike and slow wave) activity and increases in density of SMR recorded in the laboratory.

Detailed seizure frequency data were presented in only one case (Sterman and Friar, 1972) and systematic data from training sessions on emission of SMR were not presented. Nevertheless, three of the cases represent informal single-subject experiments because feedback training was discontinued after six months for a nine-week period. During this time, which constitutes the withdrawal, seizure activity showed marked increase from the previously established low levels after four to six weeks. Reintroduction of SMR biofeedback training to complete the A-B-A-B design rapidly returned patients to their improved clinical state.

Replications by other investigators

Since Sterman's reports, two other investigators in separate centers have replicated the work on SMR training for seizure disorders. By far the most impressive work has been that of Lubar and his associates (Lubar and Bahler 1976; Seifert and Lubar 1975). The eight patients had a variety of seizure disorders and had been selected by an attending neurologist to represent cases with frequent seizures, difficulty in seizure control, and high doses of anticonvulsant drugs. Included were psychomotor seizures as well as grand mal, petit mal, and other forms of seizures. All had had documented seizure disorders for at least four years and most for over 11 years.

After baseline EEG measurements and the establishment of baseline seizure frequency counts, all patients were given three sessions per week of SMR feedback training as well as binary feedback of the presence of epileptiform spike activity or slow waves. Results revealed that six of the eight patients had marked reduction in seizure frequency as well as reductions in levels of medication in some cases. In addition, the severity of the seizures that were experienced was also reduced in many cases. For the two cases for which there was no appreciable decrease in seizure frequency, the seizures experienced tended to be of lesser severity and shorter duration.

In four cases, informal single subject experiments were conducted due to patients discontinuing treatment during vacations (10 to 30 days). In three of the four "natural reversals," seizure frequency decreased from initial baseline levels when treatment was instituted and increased when it was discontinued. Reintroduction of SMR training led to a decrease in seizure frequency in three of four cases.

One of the most valuable aspects of Lubar's work has been the presentation of data on incidence of SMR in the patients' EEGs both from baseline and treatment sessions. An exact concordance between decrease in seizure frequency and increase in SMR activity would be very convincing that it is the SMR training per se which is responsible for the clinical improvement. The data were reported in terms of ratio of feedback sessions SMR to pretreatment SMR incidence. Four of the six successful patients showed evidence of increasing incidence of SMR in their EEGs as did one of the unsuccessful cases. In the other three cases there was variation around the baseline level, but no overall trend towards change.

The failure to find the exact concordance described above leaves one wondering if it is an increase in SMR in the EEG or some other aspect of the training which leads to improvement. Seizure disorders, unfortunately, are notoriously susceptible to placebo effects and other psychosocial aspects of treatment. Such effects are typically transient, however. Certainly further work is needed to pin down the key features of the training procedure.

A further replication of the value of SMR biofeedback training was provided in a report by Finley, Smith, and Etherton (1975) on the treatment of one case of frequent epileptic seizures with SMR biofeedback training. Prior to treatment, the patient, a 13-year-old male, was having approximately 75 atonic seizures per ten hours of wakefulness. His SMR percentage was 10 percent in baseline recordings. He was initially given 34 sessions of SMR feedback with the result that his seizure frequency was reduced to about one per hour and SMR percentage was up to 65 percent. He then received 45 more sessions in which feedback of epileptiform EEG activity was given. This seemed to reduce the variability in the data somewhat but led to no overall changes.

The authors, in an attempt to do a single-subject experiment, gave the subject false feedback for three sessions (trials 29–31), before returning to the true feedback training. Results of the single-subject experimental phase of treatment are difficult to interpret. There is marginal evidence of an increase in seizures and a decrease in SMR incidence during the reversal with corresponding changes after the return to treatment. However, there is so much variability in the data that one cannot be sure that changes occurred in the dependent variables coincident with changes in treatment.

In a follow-up report (Finley 1976) the patient experienced a gradual return of seizure activity and a gradual decrease of SMR activity in his EEG, despite a very prolonged period of training, approximately three times per week for six months. This same loss of beneficial effect has been reported by Sterman, MacDonald, and Stone (1974).

One report (Kaplan 1975) has failed to confirm the efficacy of SMR feedback training for the treatment of epilepsy. Kaplin treated two epileptics for three months with feedback of the SMR. Neither showed any improvement in seizure rate or any evidence of learning to produce SMR although a technique similar to Sterman's was used. Her systematic case studies thus throw some doubt on Sterman's procedure. However, her failure to obtain positive results could be due to: (1) slight modifications in the procedure including a sharper filtering system to isolate the 12–14 Hz activity than used by Sterman; (2) the idiosyncrasies of different seizure patients and of their electrophysiology, (i.e., what might work for one patient may not work for another, as Lubar had shown); (3) training may not have been long enough.

Comment. Despite Kaplan's (1975) failure to replicate the results of other workers with SMR biofeedback training, the evidence still seems fairly impressive that SMR biofeedback training can help some epileptics, especially those with frequent seizures which are poorly controlled by antiseizure medication. The systematic case studies and single-subject experiments seem to confirm this point. What is now needed is a controlled outcome study on more randomly selected seizure patients to test the utility and generality of the procedure. In such a study, a good attention placebo control condition might well be alpha biofeedback training.

5

Gastrointestinal System

Anatomy, Physiology, and Measurement

The gastrointestinal (GI) system, or tract, can be considered a long pipe, of varying diameter with several valves, or shut-off points (sphincters). The functions of the GI system are (1) transportation of nutrients and fluids into the body, (2) digestion and absorption of the nutrients and fluids, and (3) transportation of the waste products out of the body. It begins at the mouth and ends at the anus; in between lie the esophagus, stomach, intestines, and colon.

The GI tract has a coating of smooth muscle; rhythmic contractions of this muscle move food along through the tract. It is innervated by both the parasympathetic and sympathetic branches of the autonomic nervous system. The parasympathetic branch controls secretion of gastric acid, movement of the gut wall and the esophageal sphincters; the sympathetic branch controls two of the other sphincters, including the internal anal sphincter, as well as one of the muscle layers of the gut. Increased parasympathetic activity leads to increased absorption of nutrients whereas increased sympathetic activity tends to decrease GI motility and thus decreases absorption of nutrients. The final valve in the GI tract, the external anal sphincter, is striated muscle under voluntary control.

Measurement in the GI system is difficult because (1) most of it is inside the body and (2) the smooth muscle coating does not give off distinctive bioelectrical signals like the ECG of the heart. Thus measurement procedures tend to be either very invasive such as putting tubes or transducers down into the stomach, or very imprecise such as recording the electrogastrogram (EGG), a measure of rhythmic stomach contractions, from the body's surface. Probably for this reason little biofeedback research has been done with this system.

Basic Research

Stomach acid pH

Most of the basic biofeedback research with the GI system has involved training subjects to control the degree of acidity, or pH, of the contents of the stomach. The stomach contains very specialized cells which secrete a very strong acid which aids in the digestion of food. Although the lining of the stomach is fairly acid-resistant, excessive acid output can lead to ulcers. Ulcers are a fairly common problem, hence, the research into the area.

Two major reports have appeared in which pH of stomach was the response to be controlled. Welgan (1974) reported two studies in which patients with duodenal ulcers were given brief biofeedback training (one session of about 90 minutes) to control gastric acid secretions. In both studies gastric secretions were continuously aspirated via a tube into the stomach; the pH, hydrochloric acid concentration, and total volume of stomach secretions were continuously monitored.

In the first study, after a baseline period, subjects were alternately asked to decrease the acid concentration (increase pH) and to rest. Visual feedback of the pH of stomach contents was provided continuously during increase pH trials. Results showed significant increases in pH from the baseline period to the second of three experimental periods. No other significant differences were found. Thus there were no differences between experimental periods containing feedback plus instruction to change and rest periods containing contrary instructions and no feedback.

In the second study five patients were given the following sequence of 15-minutes conditions after baseline recording: rest, increase pH-1, increase pH-2; a second group of five received this sequence: increase pH-1, rest, increase pH-2. Feedback was given during increase pH trials only. Results showed significant increase in pH from baseline to the increase pH-2 condition. Overall, it seemed that instructions and feedback led to the patients being able to reduce acid concentration of the aspirated stomach contents. This control is not very specific, however.

In the second major report, Whitehead, Renault, and Goldiamond (1975) first taught four normal subjects to swallow a nasogastric tube easily. This tube contained an electrode to measure pH *in the stomach*, rather than the pH of the aspirated stomach contents as in Welgan's study. Subjects were then run in baseline sessions (5 to 13) until stability was achieved. Next they were given binary feedback of pH and instruction for a number of trials. Three of four subjects could show regular and reliable decreases in pH, i.e., increases in acid secretion. Only one of these subjects could also achieve some degree of decrease in acid secretion rate (increased pH).

Whitehead *et al.* (1975) report relatively low correlations between pH of stomach contents and pH of aspirated stomach contents. These low correlations cast some doubts on Welgan's results since the latter were obtained on aspirated stomach contents. Moreover, there is no ready mechanism in the stomach for neutralizing acid (increasing pH). The secretatory cells can either produce acid or not produce it but they do not produce a neutralizing substance.

We attempted to determine the differential effects of instructions and feedback on stomach acid pH in situ in our laboratory. Four subjects were run, two male and two female, all in good health with no history of GI disease and all in their 20s. All participated as paid volunteers.

A nasogastric (N-G) tube, similar to the one used by Whitehead *et al.* (1975), was constructed. Inside the tube was the Beckman pH electrode designed for use in the stomach itself as well as wash tubes. All subjects were run in the morning in a fasting state. After the N-G tube was put down, about 30 minutes was allowed for the stomach to come to equilibrium. The pH electrode was connected to both a Grass polygraph to provide a permanent record of the pH data and to a Beckman pH meter. There then followed a 15-minute baseline. Next came two identical sequences of four ten-minute phases: increase pH, rest and block thoughts of food, decrease pH, rest and block thoughts of food. For the first sequence, no feedback was provided to the subject. For the second sequence, analogue visual feedback, the pen movement of the pH meter, was given during the entire sequence.

Only one of the four subjects showed any consistent degree of control of stomach acid pH. Her data are presented in Fig. 5.1 as the pH reading at the end of each minute. From a baseline value of 2.0 she was able to increase pH to 2.5 without feedback. Then from a resting baseline pH of 2.8–2.9, she was able to reduce pH (increase acidity) to 1.7. Since pH is a logarithmic scale, this change represents a tenfold increase in acid concentration.

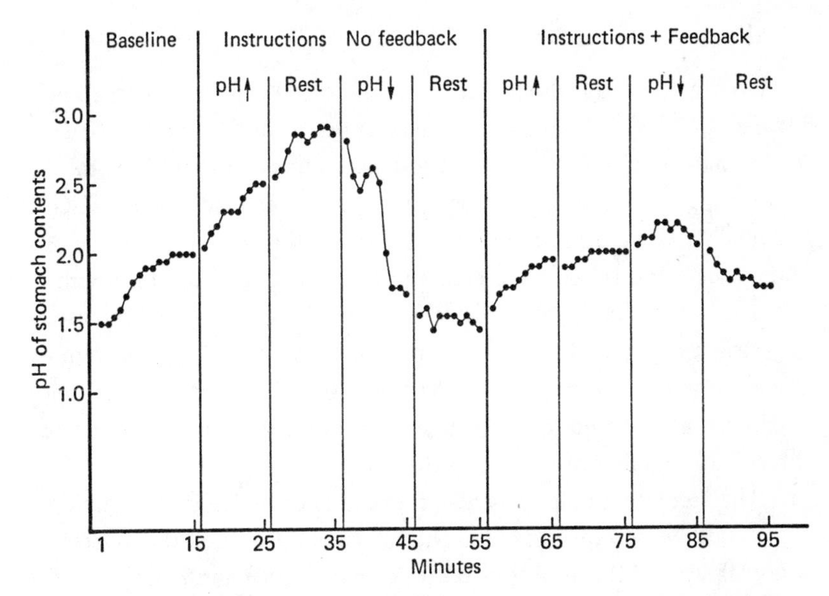

Fig. 5.1. Stomach contents pH, measured *in vitro,* as a function of experimental conditions.

When feedback was added, she increased pH from a resting baseline of 1.5 to 1.95. During the decrease pH phase, she was unsuccessful and went from 2.0 to 2.2 and back to 2.1. Thus these results showed no advantage for feedback over instructions with no-feedback in controlling stomach acid pH.

Comment. The overall impression from these data is that both ulcer patients and normals can show some changes in stomach acid pH with the help of feedback and instructions. Moreover, repeated practice seems to help. However, to date no practical application of this work has been carried out. In our opinion it will probably not prove practical to give feedback of pH directly because of the distress engendered by the monitoring. (One of us can provide direct personal testimony of the trauma. Moreover, offers of $25 for a second session did not induce any of our four subjects to return.)

Other Basic Research

Two other studies which demonstrate biofeedback effects on some aspect of GI functioning have been reported. In the first, Deckner, Hill, and Bourne (1972) sought to teach four normal subjects to control gastric motility through giving them feedback of the EGG. All subjects were run for four sessions. By the last session three of the four could reliably increase and decrease gastric motility with the aid of feedback. Since there is some relation between increased gastric motility and increase stomach acid secretion, this technique may provide a practical way of using biofeedback training for ulcer patients as opposed to the problems mentioned above in the use of feedback training of stomach acid pH.

The second study represents an example of biofeedback training of a purely visceral response. Nikoomanesh, Wells, and Schuster (1973) studied the ability of both normals ($n=3$) and patients ($n=6$) with excessive esophageal reflux to control the pressure exerted by the lower esophageal sphincter. This smooth muscle is innervated entirely by the autonomic nervous system. The lower esophageal spincter is the "valve" which controls entrance into the stomach from the esophagus; patients with esophageal reflux disorders typically show lowered ability to close this sphincter. As a result, material backs up into the esophagus from the stomach upon occasion.

The measurement is made by passing a tube containing several pressure sensitive transducers down the subject's throat. Pressure recordings were made simultaneously from three sites: esophagus, lower esophageal sphincter, and stomach. The results showed that both normal subjects and patients could increase sphincter pressure when given feedback (average increase for normals, 5.5 mm Hg; for patients, 1.5 mm Hg). These pressure increases were independent of other pressure changes and of any respiratory maneuvers. The normal subjects showed continued ability to control the pressure increase when feedback was discontinued.

Comment. These two studies represent the sparse beginnings of basic work in this field but do seem that subjects can gain control of some GI functions. So far individual effects of feedback and instructions have not been adequately assessed.

Clinical Applications

Functional diarrhea

Furman (1973) has described a simple biofeedback treatment used in treating five female patients with "functional diarrhea." This term is more or less synonymous with several others: "irritable colon," "spastic colon," or "emotional diarrhea." It is defined by the "clinical features of periodic abdominal pain and intermittent irregularity of bowel habit, usually constipation or constipation alternating with periods of normal rhythm" in the absence of specific organic pathology.

Treatment involved detecting and amplifying the naturally occurring bowel sounds (borborygmi) and then feeding this auditory signal back to the patients. This was done by placing an electronic stethoscope over the intestines and amplifying this auditory signal. The rational for this treatment was that bowel sounds were related to intestinal motility and reduced motility would lead to less eliminatory distress.

After an initial session during which the patient was familiarized with the apparatus and with listening to the sounds, each patient received a series of half-hour sessions in which she was alternately to increase and then decrease bowel sounds for four trials. Thus the training was basically discrimination training. The degree of control of bowel sounds manifested at each trial was rated on a scale from 0 to +4.

All patients reportedly showed some degree of control of bowel sounds. Moreover, all patients were reported as "now enjoying normal bowel function"; and no longer being "virtually toilet-bound." Unfortunately no systematic data are given in this report so we must rely on the author's description. Nevertheless it does seem to provide hope for this widespread disorder.

Fecal incontinence

A very embarrassing and socially debilitating GI disorder is chronic fecal incontenence. This disorder results from the patient's not having "voluntary" control of the final valve in the GI system, the external rectal sphincter.

Engel, Nikoomanesh, and Schuster (1974) reported on the biofeedback treatment of seven cases (six adults and one child) who had experienced daily fecal incontinence for three to eight years. When the external sphincter is stimulated by pressure (from a balloon inserted into the rectum and rapidly inflated), the normal reflex response is contraction of the external sphincter and relaxation of the internal sphincter. Baseline recordings from the patients, using pressure transducers, showed the reflex to be absent or greatly diminished.

In the initial stages of biofeedback training each patient was told how a normal spincter reflex reponse should appear on the polygraph record. Then the patients were given varying numbers of sessions, each of which consisted of about 50 trials on which the patient viewed the recording of their sphincter response (visual feedback) and was urged to produce a "normal" response. Patients were specifically told when they had responded appropriately. Sessions were about three weeks apart.

In the final stage of biofeedback training the patient was also given visual feedback and urged to try to produce exactly the correct response pattern between external and internal sphincter. On some trials feedback was withheld in order "to fade it out."

The principal results were patients' reports of degree of continence between sessions and at follow-up scattered over several months to several years. Four cases were complete successes with no incontinence episodes following training. Two other cases showed marked improvement; one withdrew early in treatment.

Comment. This series of systemic case studies seems to confirm the efficacy of the treatment especially since the baseline of problem behavior usually extended over several years, and improvement coincided with treatment. It certainly seems that this form of training, which could be made available in almost any well-equipped gastroenterology laboratory, should be tried before surgery or other invasive techniques are used.

Peptic ulcers

Beaty (1976) has described the biofeedback treatment of three patients with peptic ulcers. The treatment was with frontalis EMG biofeedback and regular practice in relaxation training. Ongoing records of stomach pain and medication use were obtained. Using a multiple baseline across subjects design, Beaty isolated the combination of biofeedback training, home practice in relaxation, and use of relaxation in every day situations as responsible for the marked improvement in self-report in pain and medication usage shown. Thus it appears that relaxation training assisted by biofeedback can be useful in this psychosomatic disorder.

Comment. At this point research in the use of biofeedback with GI disorders is in its infancy. However, there does seem to be some promise held out by this early work of long-range therapeutic utility.

6

Sexual Responses

This chapter will consider biofeedback research only with male sexual responses since the vast majority of the work has been with males. Male sexual response has components controlled by both branches of the autonomic nervous system. The initial phase of the male sexual response, erection, is controlled by the parasympathetic impulses which dilate the arteries and constrict the veins of the penis thus allowing arterial blood to fill the erectile tissue of the penis, causing *tumescence* or erection. The final phase of the male sexual response, ejaculation, is controlled by rhythmical sympathetic impulses. Zuckerman (1971), in a recent review of physiological indices of male sexual arousal, concluded that direct calibration of the degree of erection of the penis was the best, and only uncontaminated, measure of male sexual arousal. Several ways of measuring degree of erection have been developed; the two most practical methods involve measurement of penile circumference with either a mercury-filled rubber tube or a flexible metal ring attached to a mechanical strain gauge. Either of these two devices is then connected to an electronic circuit and the mechanical changes in the size of the penis are converted to electronic signals for recording and possible feedback. (See Abel and Blanchard 1975 for a comprehensive review.)

Basic Research

Instructional control of penile erection has been demonstrated in the absence of any biofeedback by Rubin and his associates (Laws and Rubin 1969; Henson and Rubin 1971). Both of these studies demonstrated that subjects could voluntarily inhibit the development of erections in the presence of highly erotic material to which the subject was attending.

Increasing sexual arousal

Price (1973) studied the effects of feedback on producing erection responses in normal males. Two groups listened to erotic descriptions while erection was measured. One group received both analogue and binary feedback of degree of erection and the instructions to try to get an erection; the other group received no feedback or instruction. Results showed that the feedback group showed more erection responses above a criterion level than the controls. However, the confound of instructions and feedback leaves us not knowing what led to the differences.

Decreasing sexual arousal

Rosen (1973), using a paradigm similar to that of Price, sought to determine the effects of feedback on suppression of erection elicited by erotic descriptions. All four groups heard the descriptions: three groups were instructed to suppress their erection, while the fourth just listened. One of the suppression groups received contingent binary feedback of very small changes in penile tumescence; another received false feedback, while the third received no feedback. Results, expressed as percent time during which the subject responded with more than a minimal erection, showed that the group receiving accurate feedback suppressed erection consistently more ($p<0.01$) than the other three groups which did not differ.

Clinical Applications

In the treatment of patients with sexual deviations, it has become customary, at least within the behavioral approach, to conceive of sexual deviates as possibly having a number of behavioral excesses and deficits, including excessive sexual arousal to deviant cues and possible deficits in normal heterosexual arousal, which may be independent of each other (Barlow 1974; Abel 1976).

Increasing sexual arousal

In behavioral research it is fairly customary to equate sexual arousal (verbal report) and erection response (physiological measure); most males show a high correlation between these two. To treat the problem of deficiency in normal heterosexual arousal, one needs techniques to generate, or increase, nondeviant sexual arousal. Two studies have been published in which a biofeedback procedure was used to help generate increased sexual arousal.

In the first study (Herman and Prewett 1974) a male homosexual was alternately exposed to slides of males and females while being given feedback of penile tumescence and instructions to try to generate an erection (similar to Price's 1973 study). Phases of the single-subject experiment alternated between contingent, or true, feedback, and noncontingent feedback. Erection responses, measured at independent probe sessions, showed increases in erection to both male and female stimuli, when feedback was contingent, a partial reversal when it was noncontingent, and another sustained increase when it was contingent.

This study showed that correct, or contingent, feedback led to increases in sexual arousal, to both males and females. Initial follow-up, however, revealed that the patient began engaging in homosexual behavior. Later (seven months) follow-up showed the patient had relapsed essentially to his pretreatment condition.

The second study (Barlow, Agras, Abel, Blanchard, and Young 1975) also involved treatment of male homosexuals in an effort to develop nondeviant (heterosexual) arousal. The patients were presented slides of nude females and simultaneously given analogue visual feedback of erections and instructions to try to produce erection responses.

The principal results, obtained at independent probe measurement sessions, revealed that, while patients could generate fairly large erection responses during the treatment sessions, the evidence for transfer of sexual arousal to female stimuli in the probe sessions was inconsistent. In one case there was no transfer; in the second case there was a slight increase in heterosexual arousal, while in the third there were larger increases. Control conditions in the single-subject experiments, however, indicated that exposure to the female stimuli, rather than the biofeedback training, was probably responsible for the improvement.

Decreasing sexual arousal

There have been no formal reports of the use of biofeedback to reduce deviant sexual arousal. However, informal reports from Rosen (1974) and Abel (1975, personal communication) indicate some success in teaching sexual deviates to suppress arousal to deviant cues with the aid of biofeedback, especially in exhibitionists.

Comment. At this point it seems fairly well documented by single-subject experiments that biofeedback is of little value for increasing nondeviant sexual arousal. It may be of value in teaching self-control of deviant arousal to sexual deviates, however. This would be consistent with Rosen's finding (1973) with normals that suppression of tumescence is easier to obtain than generation of tumescence.

It also seems possible that biofeedback training like that described by Price (1973) could be useful in the treatment of impotence. If one exposed the impotent patient to erotic material and provided him biofeedback, he might possibly learn to generate erections, especially as he learned to produce his own erotic fantasy.

7

Other Physiological Responses

This chapter is the last one in which the effects of biofeedback techniques on various response systems will be presented. All of the bodily responses that can be measured have not been presented in previous chapters. There are two reasons for this: first, consistent bodies of knowledge are not available for some response systems; second, the scope of this primer is of necessity limited. The reviews have been selective, and oriented toward covering response systems that are clinically important. One response system that will not be reviewed is the galvanic skin response (GSR), which has a broad research base but limited clinical application (Blanchard and Epstein 1977). The GSR was the most systematically investigated response in early biofeedback work. In fact, the majority of studies in the first review of biofeedback effects on autonomic behavior were GSR conditioning studies (Kimmel 1967). Two responses that have a limited research base, but great clinical potential, visual acuity and asthma, are briefly presented.

Visual Acuity

A small, but consistent, body of research has accumulated on the use of feedback techniques in the modification of visual acuity and accommodation. Visual acuity, or the ability of subjects to discriminate details of objects at various distances, is at least partly dependent on accommodation. Accommodation refers to modification in the curvature or thickness of the crystalline lens which changes to focus light from objects on the retina. Lens changes are determined by contraction of the ciliary muscles. Thus control of accommodation could be influenced by biofeedback training of the ciliary muscles.

Cornsweet and Crane (1973) presented the first evidence of control of accommodation by discrete verbal and auditory feedback based on continuous measurement of accommodation. Two subjects readily learned to regulate their accommodation during feedback training; next these subjects were asked to keep two lines, presented on an oscilloscope, on top of each other. The position of first line was controlled by the experimenter, while the second was controlled by the subject's accommodation. Subjects reportedly were able to perform this task.

Provine and Enoch (1975) used a slightly different methodology to study accommodation changes. The experimenters placed contact lenses on four subjects which caused stimulus objects initially to be out of focus. Changes in accommodation were necessary to bring the stimuli into focus. As visual stimuli were being presented, the experimenters presented trial-by-trial verbal feedback of changes in accommodation; the subjects also received direct visual feedback by bringing the objects in greater focus. After training, which was successful in controlling accommodation, two of the subjects were able to repeat their performance in darkness, without feedback, demonstrating true self-control.

A third example is by Malmstrom and Rundle (1976) who evaluated the effects of instructing a group of subjects to "think" an object was near, another group to think it far, as compared to a third group who simply viewed a target. The results showed differences in accommodation for the three groups, in the expected direction, with greater changes for the far group than for the watch target group, who were greater than the near group.

Giddings and Lanyon (1974) presented two studies in which changes in visual acuity in myopic subjects were shown. In the first study, four subjects were given social approval contingent upon correct visual discriminations. Contingent trials were alternated with noncontingent trials, with the performance during contingent approval superior to performance during noncontingent approval. In a second study, groups of subjects were exposed to either approval for correct discriminations, noncontingent approval presented independently of the discriminative response, or no approval for the control group. The group receiving contingent approval showed greater changes in refractive error than the other two groups, which were equal.

Based on this previous work, and some earlier work on visual retraining by ophthalmologists (Berens, Girard, Fonda, and Sells 1957), Epstein, Hannay, and Looney (1976) conducted two experiments on changing visual acuity by fading techniques in combination with contingent approval for correct visual discriminations. The fading technique involved gradually increasing the distance at which myopic subjects could discriminate visual stimuli. In a first study the fading plus reinforcement treatment was compared to a matched no-treatment control group on a measure of visual acuity. Results indicated subjects in the experimental group changed acuity significantly more than the control subjects. Six replications of a single-subject multiple baseline design were used in a second study to demonstrate the observed large-scale changes in acuity were a direct function of the fading plus reinforcement procedure. The clinical use of this procedure was then shown by Collins, Epstein, and Hannay (1976). A myopic subject with 20/40 and 20/50 vision in her two eyes was treated to improve her vision in order to pass a job screening interview that required no worse than 20/20 vision in one eye and 20/25 in the other. After approximately two months of daily training, the subject passed the physical, conducted by an independent medical examiner, with 20/20, 20/25 vision.

Asthma

Typically, respiratory behavior is assumed to be under adequate voluntary control. However, in several disorders, especially asthma, the regulation of breathing is seriously disrupted. Asthma involves narrowing of the bronchi and bronchioles (airway passages in the lungs), causing problems in inspiration and expiration of air.

The development of a biofeedback technology for asthma is, of course, dependent upon a system of measurement that provides accurate and continuous measurement of respiration. A forced oscillation technique was recently reported by Levenson (1974) which met these requirements. In addition to the description of this technology, Levenson discussed how it may be used in biofeedback research, and presents data on the use with two asthmatics in teaching them to change airway resistance (Levenson, Manuck, Strupp, Blackwood, and Snell 1974). In addition, Feldman (1976) reported decreases in respiratory resistance of four asthmatic children using analogue auditory feedback with forced oscillation measurement.

Vachon and Rich (1976) reported two studies in which a detailed analysis of feedback effects on respiratory resistance, using the forced oscillation measures of respiration, were performed. In the first study, 13 subjects were provided visual binary feedback for changes during inhalation and expiration, and then for inhalation only. Subsequently, five of the subjects were provided noncontingent feedback for respiration. The results indicated control of respiration during the first two phases, with a disruption during the noncontingent phase. In a second study, groups of subjects were exposed to either contingent or noncontingent feedback. Results of the group study were similar to those of the single-subject analysis, with appropriate and significant changes for the group receiving feedback compared to the control group. These positive effects of biofeedback on respiratory responses using the forced oscillation measurement should be contracted with the unsuccessful biofeedback procedures reported by Danker, Niklich, Pratt, and Creer (1975), using the noncontinuous less precise peak expiratory flow rate measurement of respiration.

A slightly different biofeedback approach to asthma was reported by Davis, Saunders, Creer, and Chair (1973). Based on a finding by Alexander, Niklich and Hershkoff (1972), who showed relaxation effects on peak expiratory flow rate, Davis *et al.* (1973) wanted to assess the effects of relaxation assisted by frontalis EMG feedback on peak expiratory flow rate. Twenty-four children were divided into three groups: relaxation plus feedback, relaxation, and a no-treatment control who was instructed to relax. Respiration data were taken over an eight-day baseline, five days of treatment and eight days of posttreatment; furthermore, self-reports of mood were assessed once during each of the three phases. Results indicated significant respiration changes for the nonsevere asthmatics during biofeedback assisted relaxation, and relaxation alone as compared with the control subjects, with the biggest changes in the biofeedback plus relaxation group. No maintenance of respiratory changes were observed during the posttreatment week. No relationship was observed between EMG levels and respiratory behavior. Also, no consistent treatment effects on mood were reported. This latter finding makes it difficult to assume that changes in respiration were a direct function of EMG changes.

Summary

The number of responses with which biofeedback techniques have been used are consistently increasing. In this section the applications of biofeedback for two new responses, visual acuity and asthma, were very briefly presented. The research data on both visual acuity and asthma are suggestive, and represent interesting approaches to important clinical problems.

8

A Technology for Self-Management

A major reason for the rapid growth of biofeedback is the potential for its application in the treatment of numerous clinical disorders. In the previous chapters numerous examples of the clinical use of biofeedback techniques were described. These reports have in common the control of a physiological response by the use of experimenter-controlled feedback. However, the particular strategies used to treat problem behaviors by different investigators often have little in common. Regrettably, there are no standardized protocols for treatment that are well accepted across biofeedback clinicians or researchers.

Two treatment strategies may

be used in modifying physiological responses by biofeedback. The first strategy is to attempt to produce a long-term, tonic change in the affected response system. This strategy assumes that within-session changes will endure between sessions. Thus, long-term changes outside of the laboratory can be obtained that are a function of the laboratory training procedures. One excellent example of this strategy has been reported by Sterman (1973) in his pioneering EEG work with epileptic patients. Sterman brought epileptic patients to his laboratory for regular, i.e., three times per week, training to produce the 12–14 Hz rhythm in the sensorimotor cortex (SMR) which had previously been demonstrated to inhibit seizures in research with cats. He assumed that semipermanent changes in brain functioning may be produced by the feedback training such that the electrical discharges associated with seizures will not occur after extended biofeedback training. This assumption was supported by an observed reduction in seizure rate, a normalization of resting and sleep EEG, and EEG control as a function of feedback. Sterman did not instruct his patients to do anything outside of the lab which might inhibit seizures, since he believed his laboratory feedback was producing a semipermanent change in brain functioning which would last from session to session. In fact, seizures did not return to their initial rate in his first set of patients until three months after the termination of treatment.

The second treatment strategy is probably more common, and involves teaching the client to control problem behavior when it occurs. Procedures in which the client can change behavior without external assistance are often called self-management techniques (Thoresen and Mahoney 1974). In self-management strategies the client is taught techniques which can be used to change abnormal responses. For example, a patient could be trained to reduce muscle tension when a headache is impending, or to reduce heart rate in the early stages of an anxiety attack associated with tachycardia. The technique of having the client control behavior is most appropriate for phasic disorders, or ones in which problems occur intermittently such that the target physiological response is not always at abnormal levels. Phasic disorders may be contrasted with chronic disorders, such as hypertension, in which an abnormal level of responding is the rule, rather than the exception. Chronic disorders require permanent tonic changes in the problem responses for an appropriate treatment effect. Phasic disorders do not require a permanent change, but rather the problem response needs to be controlled only during an attack.

The remainder of this chapter will discuss ways to evaluate the ability of the client to self-manage behaviors and a technology for training clients in self-management of problem behaviors.

Self-Management

The goal of a therapist treating a client with a phasic disorder is to teach the client to regulate the problem response whenever changes in the target response are detrimental to physical, cognitive, or motoric functioning. As a rule this regulation must be accomplished outside of the laboratory and without the equipment used for training. Thus, one necessary assessment is that the problem response systems of the client be controlled without *feedback*. The simplest technique to use in doing this is to provide instructions for the client to change a response, but not to provide feedback (Brener 1974). The instructions may be presented in numerous ways, including verbal (Blanchard and Scott 1974) or visual (Levene, Engel, and Pearson 1973) cues by the experimenter, or even verbal cues given by the subject (Blanchard and Scott 1974). The degree of control can be established by evaluating the effects of various instructional conditions. Can a client increase and decrease a system when instructed, or can the client produce changes only in one direction? Also, can the client produce regulated changes, or only changes of one magnitude. For example, can he or she increase heart rate five beats, and then 10 to 15, or do all his or her efforts result in a five-beat change. Certainly the quality of self-management will be a function of the degree of control over the system in question.

The second assessment should be whether the changes can be produced outside of the laboratory without feedback. Of course one potential problem with this evaluation is obtaining an accurate measurement of the response in the natural environment. This may not be a problem for some responses as heart rate (Bell and Schwartz 1975), since anyone can be trained to take a pulse, or for blood pressure, as sphygmomanometers (blood pressure devices) are relatively portable. However EMG or EEG activity may be difficult to measure outside of the laboratory without telemetry. Telemetry involves the transmission of physiological signals from transmitters on moving subjects to stationary recording equipment. The widespread use of this equipment for clinical problems is at present reduced by the expense of the equipment and relatively short-range transmission capabilities.

Definition of Self-Management

While self-management techniques have been applied only recently to physiological responses, they have a longer history in the management of cognitive and motoric responses. A voluminous literature on basic and applied self-management research (Thoresen and Mahoney 1974) has developed, complemented by rigorous thinking regarding the important events that control or influence self-management (Bandura 1971; Thoresen and Mahoney 1974). While numerous theoretical conceptions are available, the authors favor a behavioral approach to self-management, which is the prominent approach, and the position that has certainly contributed the most research.

A basic assumption of the behavioral approach is that all behaviors are subject to certain principles. A second assumption is that behavior does not occur randomly, but rather is reliably influenced by events that occur in the person's immediate environment (an environment which includes internal stimuli). Much of treatment is thus a search for the events that currently control a problem behavior with the subsequent attempt to rearrange the controlling events. If you assume all behavior is controlled, then it is useful to identify the source of control. Control may arise either from the environment, acting relatively independently of the person, or as a function of that person manipulating the events that influence the person's life. The first type of control is external, or experimenter-managed, while the latter is self-managed. Thus a main difference between external and self-management is the agent who manipulates the events that control the behavior. Self-management occurs when a person manipulates events that reliably influence behavior. Self-management is not assumed to be merely a function of willpower of self-determination. Rather, to self-manage behavior it may be necessary to learn skills to analyze and interact with one's environment.

Since the agent of control is an important factor in differentiative external and self-management, we may derive the necessary components of self-control from an analysis of procedures used in external control. In order to use external control to influence the behavior of another person several things are necessary. First, we must be able to observe and record samples or sequences of ongoing behavior, such that we can detect changes in the target behavior. Secondly, we must be able to identify a procedure that reliably influences a behavior. For example, if we want to increase rate of a behavior, we may present a positive reinforcer after the response occurs, or remove a negative reinforcer. Finally, we must arrange the sequencing of the controlling events in such a way so as to obtain and maintain the ideal response topography and rate necessary for the effect. Thus, we must be able to observe the response, develop a strategy for changing it, and implement the strategy in such a manner which will produce a lasting effect. Similar components are necessary for self-management.

Self-monitoring

Self-monitoring is the first component that may be necessary for adequate self-management. Self-monitoring involves both self-observation and self-recording. Self-observation is the process whereby a person observes his or her own behavior, and self-recording involves making a permanent record of the observations.

Why is self-monitoring necessary? One obvious reason is that a person cannot regulate something unless he or she knows when it occurs. If persons are asked to increase the number of times they tap their fingers on a tabletop, they can easily accommodate because they have peripheral sensation and visual observation of their fingers tapping and can thus know their rates over a time period by using self-observation and recording. However, if persons are asked to increase their heart rates, they may find this request a different matter because they may not know how fast their hearts are beating at any time, or even what a heartbeat feels like. Thus, they would not know whether the heart rate is increasing, decreasing, or staying the same.

A second reason for self-monitoring is to provide a record of behaviors for evaluation of treatment effects that may be accessible to observation by the subject only. For example, it may be impossible for the experimenter to observe and record various physiological responses of the subject during the subjects time outside the laboratory. Such observation and recording probably can be performed by the subject only.

A third reason may be due to the reactive effects associated with self-monitoring. When used with overt responses, self-monitoring is typically associated with reliable changes of the monitored response over short periods. There is considerable research on the effects of monitoring high rate overt behaviors such as cigarette smoking and eating certain foods. Results consistently indicate the short-term effects of monitoring to be a decrease in response rate (Kazdin 1974). There is some reason to expect self-monitoring a physiological response to regulate its rate, as demonstrated recently for blood pressure (Carnahan and Nugent 1975). Self-monitoring of blood pressure in hypertensives produced a decrease in systolic pressure of 7.5 mm Hg.

Self-control

In addition to detecting a problem response, the person must be able to reliably influence the response when necessary. The typical cue for the person to begin self-control is the detection of the beginning stages of problem occurrence. For example, the person may want to start to decrease forehead muscle tension at the initial onset of muscle tightness, well before a headache occurs. Furthermore, it may be easier to reduce tension levels at this time, and the person may thus be able to prevent a headache from occurring.

There are numerous strategies of self-control, a strategy being defined in terms of what the subject actually is doing when feedback is not available to reliably influence the problem response. However, it is not presently clear how strategies are developed or what the strategies are. It is tempting to assume that strategies for decreasing a physiological response involve some form of relaxation, while increasing a response involves some tension. It does not appear these issues are that simple, as Kristt and Engel (1975) have shown, blood pressure decreases are independent of numerous physiological indices of relaxation. Also Epstein, Hersen, and Hemphill (1974) demonstrated decreases in muscle tension to be independent of heart rate changes, a common measure of relaxation. Let it suffice to say that subjects can learn to develop reliable strategies that are useful in modifying certain bodily states but cannot tell you what they are when asked. Some of the most important work in basic psychophysiology is attempting to find out what the subjects are doing to regulate physiological responses. An excellent example of identifying a controlling strategy was recently performed by Plotkin (1976), who clearly showed control of EEG alpha production to be a function of oculomotor activity.

Self-reinforcement

After it is established that the person knows when to change a bodily response, and has a strategy to do it, it is important that the person is reliable and consistent in using the strategy. This may seem an unimportant component for some problems, particularly those involving pain. The removal of pain by engaging in the strategy may be sufficient to maintain using the strategy. While this may be true, often the presence of pain indicates the attack is in the final stages and then may be very difficult to control, as in migraine headaches. In such cases the pain must be prevented. If this is the case, the task for the subject now becomes one in which he or she is to interrupt ongoing activities when he or she is nonsymptomatic is order to prevent the occurrence of the disorder. While research is not now available on how consistent people are in complying with these types of requests, widespread individual differences will probably be found between subjects in compliance rates.

In addition to disorders that produce pain, there are several important problems that are asymptomatic. During treatment of these problems persons must control bodily processes on the good faith that they are improving their health, because they cannot detect any differences between health and lack of health. Hypertension is such a disorder, and compliance is poor for hypertension medication regimens. This is somewhat surprising, as medication taking is not time consuming nor interruptive of ongoing behaviors. It is possible that requiring a client to engage in the relatively time-consuming tasks involved in biofeedback may produce an even more difficult compliance problem. However, the use of these procedures may have one advantage over medicine treatment. Biofeedback techniques may produce some positive side effects, as the person may enjoy the relaxing effects produced by biofeedback and practice to obtain those effects. In comparison, the person may get no satisfaction, or notice no changes while taking medicine.

Now that we have described the components of self-management, it is appropriate to develop a technology, or a set of procedures that can reliably be used to teach persons to regulate bodily responses on their own instruction without external feedback.

A Technology of Self-Management

In this section, training techniques that could result in self-management are presented. The authors make no assertion that these are the best or only ways to proceed. Arrangement of these techniques in a different sequence, or the development of new techniques may be superior.

The most important component of self-management is *self-control.* Without this component the discrimination and self-maintenance phases are unimportant. The traditional way to develop self-control is to begin with external or feedback-influenced control so that reliable regulation of the response is possible with the experimenter, or therapist, manipulating all of the important events. Then subjects are periodically tested without external feedback to assess if they have developed some strategies for self-control. The specific techniques for going from external to self-control have received surprisingly little attention. However, there are several standard techniques for maintaining control of behavior with reductions in feedback or reinforcer contact. These involve gradually reducing (fading) the amount of feedback the subjects receive.

During the initial stages of training subjects are provided feedback of their behavior continuously. The relationship between their response rate and rate of a reinforcer or feedback presentation, formally stated as a contingency, can be rearranged so that eventually no feedback is provided, with no appreciable decrease in response rate. Consider changing the feedback arrangement in a heart-rate control test so that instead of getting feedback on a beat-by-beat basis the subjects get it every other beat, and then every third beat, with changes made gradually until they require feedback on an intermittent basis only. At a certain point the contact with the feedback has been reduced so much that it can be removed without any deleterious effects. Thus, it is probable that feedback, when removed gradually enough and under carefully monitored conditions, can be faded out, or withdrawn, with no resultant decrease in control of the behavior.

A similar technique might be to reduce the feedback on a time, rather than response, basis. For example, initial feedback could be provided continuously for several sessions, and then be withdrawn for one minute out of every five minutes. If the behavior does not deteriorate, then the therapist progresses to two out of five minutes with this strategy eventually ending in the total withdrawal of feedback.

While these techniques are reasonable, it may not always be necessary to gradually reduce the feedback. Rather, a person may obtain a self-control strategy quickly, so feedback may be withdrawn abruptly. The best way to bridge the gap between feedback and no feedback conditions has received very little research attention. Most basic research studies have simply compared behavior during feedback and nonfeedback states, with no attention paid to fading out feedback. However, an exemplary example of the use of fading was presented by Weiss and Engel (1971). These experimenters were training patients with premature ventricular contractions to increase, decrease, and regulate their heart rates. Their procedures involved changing of the feedback availability from a continuous, to one out of two minutes, to one out of every four to one out of every eight minutes. Good maintenance of control was observed with the reduced feedback.

Discrimination

After subjects can reliably influence their response without feedback, i.e., demonstrate self-control, it is important to ensure that they know when to control the response. They must be able to *discriminate* among the situations that require them to begin self-control. Of course, it is possible to bypass discrimination if the therapist arranges for the subjects to practice the techniques at regular intervals throughout the day, for example before breakfast and after dinner. When self-control is not practiced on a pain or abnormal response contingent basis, the therapist expects to modify or prevent the occurrence of any abnormal states.

There are several classes of physiological responses that produce different amounts of feedback to the person that may facilitate or impede discrimination. The first class includes responses that produce pain. These include both tension and migraine headaches. The pain is an easily discriminable event such that subjects usually need not be trained to detect it, but can engage in their self-control strategy, on a pain contingent basis, when pain begins.

A second class of physiological responses do not produce pain when they change, but the changes are easily discriminable by self-monitoring technques. For example, heart rate is easily detected by monitoring the peripheral pulse, and respiration rate may be easily counted. Any response that can be monitored by self-observation or by use of a portable measurement device will fall in this category.

The final class of physiological responses are those that are generally silent, or do not produce any easily discriminable peripheral sensation. A typical response of this type is EEG activity. Another may be blood pressure, which is one reason why hypertension is considered to be such a dangerous disease.

When therapists are trying to teach a patient to detect something that produces pain, as a headache, or that is easily detected by self-observation techniques, as tachycardia, they should have few problems. However, a technology must be developed for teaching people to discriminate responses such as blood pressure, that have few natural sensory consequences.

Since this is a discrimination issue, the procedures used to produce discrimination of exteroceptive (rather than the interoceptive discussed now) stimuli may be appropriate. The majority of work in this very new area has been on heart rate, with investigations using such diverse paradigms as free operant (Epstein and Stein 1974), free trials (Epstein, Cinciripini, McCoy, and Marshall 1977) and matching-to-sample (Brener and Jones 1974), techniques. All of these investigations have been performed in laboratories; however, it would be easy to extend the laboratory methodology to the natural environment. The procedures that will be described in detail are the free trials procedures used by Epstein *et al.* 1977, since it is the authors' opinion these are most adaptable to general, extra-laboratory use.

The first step in the procedure used by Epstein *et al.* (1977, Study II) was to obtain a measure of heart rate, and then arrange for certain heart-rate levels to be positive stimuli, and other levels negative stimuli. A positive stimulus was one that indicated a subject should respond, while a negative stimulus was one that indicated the subject should not respond. The heart rate levels selected were those on either side of the subject's mean rate during the initial part of the session. In this way about half of the time the subject was presented with positive stimuli, while the other half of the time the subject was presented with negative stimuli. Each of six subjects was presented with two response buttons. During a short trial, subjects were to estimate whether their heart rates were above or below their mean level. They were instructed to respond on one button if the heart rate was above its mean level, and respond on the other button if the heart was below the mean level. There were two phases in the experiment, baseline and training, implemented in a multiple baseline fashion. The training conditions included trial-and-error procedure for one-half of the subjects, and fading procedures for the other half. Results indicated low levels of discriminations during baseline, with clear improvements as a function of training. No clear differences were apparent between changes in discriminations produced by trial-and-error and fading procedure.

The extension of this technology to the natural environment would be relatively simple. Consider the problem of detecting blood pressure increases in a hypertensive. First, the accurate measurement of blood pressure must be provided several times a day, and these measures must be taken over a week period to establish baseline levels of blood pressure. Then the midpoint of this distribution must be calculated and anything greater than the mean must be defined as an increase, anything less than the mean, as a decrease. Subjects are instructed to tell whether their blood pressure is higher or lower than normal on each measurement occasion. During a first phase, the subjects' feedback is the accuracy of their discriminative response. Correct responses are reinforced by social praise. While this study has not yet been performed, it is likely these procedures would produce correct detection of blood pressure levels. If anyone actually desires to put this analysis to empirical test, it would be important to control for the activities engaged in prior to blood pressure measurement each day.

Self-maintenance

The final consideration in self-management is self-maintenance. Concern for self-maintenance is appropriate when subjects have a self-control strategy, and know when to implement it. Then it is important for them to continue to use the strategy. This may not be a problem for people who implement the strategy to reduce or prevent pain. Such people are adequately reinforced for their efforts by the reduction of pain. However, the problem of getting people to comply with a treatment regimen which does not produce any relief from pain may be difficult. Telling people that it is important to regulate their blood pressure for their future health, when they do not feel bad when their blood pressure is high, and do not feel any better when their pressure is low, may prove to be a difficult problem. The emphasis on preventing a future problem is reasonable, and people will agree to the rationale, but may have trouble actually changing their everyday behavior to reduce something they do not find aversive.

The techniques for producing self-maintenance of behavior are perhaps the most researched in the entire area of self-managing overt and motoric behavior. It is likely that these principles could be generalized to maintaining self-management of physiological behavior. A complete set of these strategies is available in the excellent book on self-management by Thoresen and Mahoney (1974). An example of maintenance strategy will be presented to illustrate principles.

Assume a person is diagnosed as having hypertension and has been instructed by a doctor to lower the blood pressure. The person is brought into the laboratory and a biofeedback strategy based on the constant cuff technique issued to lower the blood pressure. The initial analysis indicates that the person's pressure can be reliably lowered by the technique. The person is taught a self-managed procedure to use a sphygmomanometer as Kristt and Engel (1975) have done. The therapist finds out that soon after the person stops formal training blood pressure increases again. The person's spouse reports that the self-control exercises have been abandoned. At this point it may be appropriate to develop an external control procedure that will regulate the person's practice of the procedure. For example, the therapists may request that the client deposit $100, to be returned in $25 installments each week that blood pressure remains low.

A next phase may be to fade from externally managed to self-managed compliance. A self-managed technique could be set up whereby the client chooses something he or she likes to do each evening, such as watch TV, and it is arranged so that the activity can be engaged in only after the practice of biofeedback. It is probable that to ensure maintenance of self-management occasional external reinforcers would be necessary, such as praise from the client's spouse for reliably practicing. In the event that self-management strategies are not sufficient to maintain self-control, the use of external control could be continued.

Summary

The basis for most biofeedback approaches is to teach the client self-management skills. While very little research has been performed on techniques that can be used to facilitate self-management of physiological responses, there is a considerable body of literature on self-management of motoric and congitive responses. Based on this literature, procedures for assessing and producing the components of self-management were outlined. These components include detecting when to begin self-management, instituting a self-control strategy, and the applications of self-maintenance techniques.

9

Issues and Future Directions

In this last chapter we will discuss several issues such as mediation which cut across several organ or response systems. We will also speculate a bit as to some future directions for biofeedback.

Mediation

Previous discussions in this book have clearly shown that feedback may be arranged to reliably influence a selected target response. However, demonstrations that a selected target response changes does not conclusively show that the feedback was operating exclusively on the selected response. This is an important problem for psychophysiological researchers since the response systems within the body are interrelated. For example, assume that heart rate is responsive to respiration or muscle changes, such that subjects may control their heart by changing their respiration rate or depth of breathing. Observations of heart rate change as a function of respiration change would indicate that heart rate is not being directly controlled, and could invalidate the idea that autonomic behavior can be operantly conditioned. For these reasons, a significant amount of attention has been directed to mediation problems, discussed initially by Katkin and Murray (1968).

One necessary precursor to evaluation of mediation is demonstration of a correlational relationship between two responses. For example, if high heart rate and increases in respiration rate are positively correlated, it would be reasonable to assess the role of respiration increases in producing heart rate changes. While correlational procedures may indicate relationships between responses, they cannot be used to study whether changes in a mediator's response are the direct cause of changes in the target response. However, there have been numerous experimental procedures developed to assess the role of mediation in producing changes in various response systems.

The first procedure is to control the mediator, such that changes in the target response can be observed, *independent* of changes in the mediator. For example, if heart rate is observed to increase and decrease while respiration rate and depth are controlled, it can be assumed that changes in respiration are not crucial to observed heart rate control. In research with rats, this has been accomplished by paralyzing the rats using curare and then artificially respirating the animals, precisely controlling their respiration. The use of curare also has the effect of controlling the effects of changes in peripheral muscular responses, which have also been assumed to mediate autonomic changes. Numerous feedback influenced changes have been observed for autonomic responses in curarized rats including heart rate (DiCara and Miller 1968a; Trowill 1967) and blood pressure (DiCara and Miller 1968b).

In research with humans it is difficult to curarize a subject. In the only published example, Birk, Crider, Shapiro, and Tursky (1966) did observe operant control of GSR in a curarized subject. A simpler procedure may be to ask subjects to regulate the suspected mediating response system, by providing cues to assist in regulation of the mediator. If respiration effects are to be ruled out, the subject may be instructed to regulate rate and depth during the conditioning of heart rate (Brener and Hothersall 1967), or may be provided a flashing light to which the respiration rate can be matched (Sroufe 1969). Or a subject could be directly trained to regulate the mediator through feedback (Epstein, Malone, and Cunningham 1976), so that one feedback source was being used to regulate the mediator while the target response was controlled by another feedback source. Feedback might also be available in a compound schedule which provided an event contingent on the regulation of the mediator and changes in the target response.

There are several other procedural ways to arrange feedback for the mediator and/or target response that can evaluate the importance of the mediator to changes in the target responses. Assume changes in an autonomic response, such as GSR, are assumed to be a function of changes in skeletal responding, and feedback delivery is often contingent upon concurrent changes in both responses. If the skeletal muscle responses are responsible for GSR control, then a large disruption in control should be apparent if GSR responses are reinforced in the *absence* of muscle responding. However, if GSR control is observed in the absence of muscle activity, the importance of this mediator can be quickly ruled out, as demonstrated by Rice (1966).

A similar strategy was used recently in studying blood pressure discrimination (Martin and Epstein 1976). Discriminative responding to blood pressure decreases was observed to be a function of feedback in the two subjects studied. However, momentary blood pressure changes appeared to be correlated with respiration patterns, such that blood pressure decreases were often produced during inspirations. Thus, the discrimination response often occurred during the compound stimulus of respiration inspiration/blood pressure decrease. The importance of inspiration was evaluated by reinforcing correct responding only when blood pressure decreased at any time within the respiration cycle other than during inspirations. Results indicated discrimination was maintained during this control procedure.

Another tactic would be to arrange feedback specifically for the mediator while observing changes in the target. If the mediator actually was responsible for control of the target response, directly reinforcing and increasing the rate of the mediator should improve control of the target response. For example, if it is suspected that deep breaths are critical for production of GSR activity, reinforcing deep breaths should increase GSR rate. However, when Gavalas (1968) attempted this, she found control of respiration with habituation of GSR responding. These data show that the feedback contingency in GSR studies was not simply producing GSR changes through the reinforcement of deep respirations, even though deep breathing will produce GSRs.

Mediation issues were studied in a refreshingly new way in an excellent series of studies on response patterning reported by Schwartz (1974). The studies evaluated the relationship between heart rate and blood pressure changes by arranging contingencies in several ways for both responses. A subject could be reinforced for integration of the two systems when changes in heart rate and blood pressure were in the same direction, or be reinforced for differentiation when heart rate and blood pressure were in opposite directions. These procedures provide for the analysis of mediation by assessing the degree to which the two responses are independent or related. For example, if heart rate directly mediated blood pressure, and heart rate changes were the primary cause for blood pressure changes, then it would be impossible to cause heart rate to increase and blood pressure to decrease.

The initial studies in the series assessed the effect of systolic blood pressure modification on heart rate (Shapiro, Tursky, Gershon, and Stern 1969) and the effect of heart rate changes on systolic blood pressure (Shapiro, Tursky, and Schwartz 1970). Both studies showed the target responses could be controlled, but no significant systematic effects were observed on the other responses.

Schwartz, Shapiro, and Tursky (1971) then assessed the effects of a contingency arranged to reinforce integrated heart rate and blood pressure change. Five subjects were reinforced for heart rate /blood pressure increases, while five others were reinforced for heart rate/blood pressure decreases. Results were appropriate to the contingencies, with better changes for subjects reinforced for decreasing both responses. Schwartz (1972) replicated the integration finding across twenty subjects, and also assessed the differentiation of the two responses by reinforcing heart rate increases/blood pressure decreases and heart rate decrease/blood pressure increase. The results indicated reliable effects on integration, with decreases again being larger than increases. The subjects reinforced for decreasing BP and increasing HR showed evidence for learning. The task requiring increasing BP and decreasing HR was more difficult. Though the changes were in the appropriate direction, they were not significantly different. The results of these studies show a specificity of the operation of the reinforcement contingencies on two cardiovascular responses as closely related as heart rate and blood pressure. These data certainly indicate that heart rate and blood pressure are at least relatively independent, and change in one does not necessarily cause change in the other. This is important because in single-target response studies contingencies may operate coincidentally on two responses that are naturally correlated in time, as heart rate and blood pressure.

Schwartz (1974) has outlined a model for the prediction and control of physiological responses based on results obtained in these patterning studies, and on his recent research findings. The model incorporates both environmental contingency and biological constraint factors, and may be able to provide predictions for what responses are easiest to change, and the degree of change possible in various systems. A strong emphasis is placed on observation of the natural relationships in time between the two responses. For example, Schwartz predicted it would be easier to produce integration of heart rate and blood pressure than differentiation, since heart rate and blood pressure tend to increase and decrease together during precontingency manipulations. The results of his research were consistent with his prediction.

The previous discussion of mediation has been addressed to basic research strategies designed to show the cause for change in the target response was not really the change in a mediating response, which might be easier to control than the target response. While this was an important point for basic research, current basic and applied researchers are attacking the mediation issue different. It can be assumed that one isolated response in the body is not likely to change without some related system influencing the change, and a profitable line of research is thus to identify what strategy the subject *does* use in producing change (Schwartz 1976). In other words, attempts are now being made to identify, rather than rule out, important physiological relationships. In addition, a number of investigators have attempted to utilize the power of mediation to produce changes in related systems. For example, Epstein and Webster (1975); Harris, Katkin, Lick, and Hubberfield (1976), and Sroufe (1971) have all emphasized the possibilities of using respiration control to mediate control of autonomic responses. Patel, in an interesting series of studies, has shown excellent control of blood pressure in hypertensives by controlled breathing and GSR biofeedback (Patel 1973; Patel 1975; Patel and North 1975). As Schwartz

(1974) has indicated, early research on mediation trying "to blame autonomic learning on something else" was not as productive in understanding the processes involved in control of autonomic responses as current research approaches designed to identify the psychophysiological variables that do control changes in physiological response.

Biofeedback: The Ultimate Weapon?

As we noted in the first chapter of this book, the list of disorders which have been "successfully" treated with biofeedback is ever expanding. For example, two recent reports describe the successful treatment of atopic dermatitis (skin rash) (Haynes 1976) and hyperkinesis in a child (Lubar and Shouse 1976). It is thus theoretically possible to treat an ever-widening range of disorders: for any problem for which there are neural connections between the CNS and the response effector, it may be possible to design a biofeedback treatment.

What appears to be an especially prevalent trend in this continually expanding range of application of biofeedback is the use of EMG frontalis feedback to treat a wide range of what might be termed "stress-related problems" such as ulcers, dermatitis, and hypertension. Perhaps biofeedback is the "ultimate weapon." Or is it?

Hard on the heels of these newly described uses of biofeedback training has come a new generation of research reports in which biofeedback training is compared with some form of relaxation training. For example there have been reports comparing biofeedback training with relaxation training in the treatment of tension headaches (Cox *et al.* 1975), migraine headaches (Blanchard *et al.* 1977) and hypertension (Shoemaker and Tasto 1975). In all of these comparisons the same results obtain: both biofeedback training and relaxation training lead to significant clinical improvement but there is no advantage for one form of treatment over the other. We suspect that, as this second generation of studies involving stress-related disorders is conducted, similar results will continue to be found.

To us the inescapable conclusion which can be drawn from the data to date is that many forms of biofeedback, especially frontalis EMG feedback, is one of a number of ways of teaching people to relax. In fact, one of the most active areas of research in psychology and in medicine may well become the development of nonpharmacological, noninvasive means of combatting stress, particularly excessive sympathetic arousal or excessive elicitation of the *defense–alarm* response.

Relaxation, very broadly conceived, seems to be the *final common pathway* to the clinical benefits. This idea is very similar to Stoyva and Budzynski's notion (1974) of the generalized benefits of "cultivated low arousal." Biofeedback training thus seems to be one of a number of means of achieving the same result. Only future research will show if it is the best or most efficient means. At present it can claim only to be the most widely publicized.

We do not mean, however, to dismiss all of clinical biofeedback as just one other form of relaxation training. In certain areas where the patient needs to learn to control a particular physiological response, such as in muscle reeducation, the control of fecal incontinence, or reduction of seizures, biofeedback training certainly involves more than teaching the patient to relax. Only further research will determine if it has an advantage or not, and if it is the *ultimate weapon* or not.

It will probably be the case that biofeedback training will follow other forms of psychological treatment to the extent that the optimum situation will be knowing whether certain forms of biofeedback are better suited to certain patients with certain disorders than any other form of treatment. Such a high level of specificity would seem to be a logical long-range goal.

The Future of Biofeedback

It is difficult to predict the future for a field like biofeedback which is still in its adolescence. In the near future, even as this book is being written and printed, new clinical uses of biofeedback training will undoubtedly be described in the professional journals. Many of these uses will be in the area of helping patients reduce excessive sympathetic arousal and its concomitant effects as described above.

Predictions for a longer time span are more difficult. One trend which seems likely to continue is the evaluation of biofeedback-training techniques in a more rigorous manner through conducting controlled-group outcome studies. This type of work is difficult but necessary in order to put this field in its proper perspective. We would hope that as these studies are conducted, they will include a comparison with some form of relaxation training so that the additional benefits, if any, of specific physiological feedback can be assessed.

Another line of research which may develop is the use of biofeedback training to obtain a particular physiological state so that the effects of that state on other physiological responses can be determined. More specifically, biofeedback training offers a noninvasive and highly reversible way of obtaining specific physiological states. This is in contrast to obtaining that state, in human subjects, through administering drugs. Once the desired state is obtained, one can study its effects on other physiological systems.

An example of this kind of research was recently completed in our laboratory. We (Young, Langford, and Blanchard 1976) sought to determine the relationship between HR acceleration and the output of a certain substance, *renin*, which helps regulate blood pressure, into the blood stream. Baseline heart rates and plasma renin activity (PRA) levels were initially determined for three sessions. Next the male subject, a paid volunteer, was taught to increase his HR with the assistance of biofeedback for a series of daily 30-minute trials; he achieved increases of about 30 BPM sustained over the entire session. Blood samples to determine PRA were drawn immediately before and after the HR acceleration and showed a clear-cut relationship between PRA levels and HR acceleration. The main value of the study, however, was to demonstrate a technology for using biofeedback training to study other systems.

As a final speculation it may be that any response which can be classically conditioned, including such things as presence of clotting factor in the blood, can also be brought under biofeedback control. The limiting conditions appear to be (1) the ability to measure moment to moment changes in the response system and (2) some sort of neural connections between the response system and the CNS. Within the limits imposed by these two conditions the range of biofeedback effects may be very great and the extent of "mind-body" interactions profound. Only future research will tell.

References

Aarons, L. 1971. Subvocalization: aural and EMG feedback in reading. *Percept. Mot. Skills* **33**: 271–306.

Abel, G.G., and E.B. Blanchard 1976. The measurement and generation of sexual arousal in male sexual deviates. In M. Hersen, R.M. Eisler, and P.M. Miller (eds.), *Progress in behavior modification*. New York: Academic Press, Vol. II.

Alexander, A.B. 1975. An experimental test of assumptions related to the use of electromyogram biofeedback as a general relaxation training technique. *Psychophysiol.* **12**: 656–662.

———, C.A. French, and N. Goodman 1975. A comparison of auditory and visual feedback in biofeedback assisted muscular relaxation training. *Psychophysiol.* **12**: 119–123.

———, D.R. Niklich, and H. Hershkoff, 1972. The immediate effects of systematic relaxation training on peak expiratory flow rates in asthmatic children. *Psychosom. Med.* **34**: 388–394.

Amato, A., C.A. Hermsmeyer, and K.M. Kleinman 1973. Use of electromyographic feedback to increase inhibitory control of spastic muscles. *Phys. Ther. Rev.* **53**: 1063–1066.

Anand, B.K., G.S. Chhina, and B. Singh 1961. Some aspects of electroencephalographic studies in yogies. *Electroenceph. clin. Neurophysiol.* **13**: 452–456.

Andrews, J.M. 1964. Neuromuscular re-education of the hemiplegic with the aid of the electromyograph. *Arch. phys. Med. Rehabil.* **45**: 530–532.

Bandura, A. 1971. Vicarious and self-reinforcement processes. In R. Glaser (ed.), *The nature of reinforcement*. New York: Academic, pp. 228–278.

Barlow, D.H. 1974. The treatment of sexual deviation: toward a comprehensive behavioral approach. In Calhoun *et al.* (eds.), *Innovative treatment methods in psychopathology*. New York: Wiley, pp. 121–147.

_____, W.S. Agras, G.G. Abel, E.B. Blanchard, and L.D. Young 1975. Biofeedback and reinforcement to increase heterosexual arousal in homosexuals. *Behav. Res. Ther.* **13**: 45–50.

Basmajian, J.V. 1963a. Conscious control of single nerve cells. *New Scient.* **369**: 662–664.

_____ 1963b. Control and training of individual motor units. *Science* **141**: 440–441.

_____ 1967. Control of individual motor units. *Amer. J. Phys. Med.* **46**: 480–486.

_____ 1972. Electromyography comes of age. *Science* **176**: 603–609.

_____ 1967. *Muscles alive*. Baltimore: Williams and Wilkins.

_____, M. Baeza, and C. Fabrigar 1965. Conscious control and training of individual spinal motorneurons in normal human subjects. *J. new Drugs* **5**: 78–85.

_____, C. G. Kukulka, M.G. Narayan, and K. Takebe 1975. Biofeedback treatment of foot-drop after stroke compared with standard rehabilitation techniques: effects on voluntary control and strength. *Arch. phys. Med. Rehabil.* **56**: 231–236.

_____, and J. Samson 1973. Standardization of methods in single motor unit training. *Am. J. phys. Med.* **52**: 250–256.

_____, and T. G. Simard 1967. Effects of distracting movements on the control of trained motor units. *Amer. J. Phys. Med.* **46**: 1427–1449.

Beaty, E. T. 1976. *Feedback-assisted relaxation training as a treatment for gastric ulcers.* Paper presented at 7th annual meeting of Biofeedback Research Society, Colorado Springs.

Bell, I. R., and G. E. Schwartz 1973. *Individual factors in bidirectional voluntary control and reactivity in human heart rate.* Paper presented at meeting of Western Psychological Association, Anaheim, April.

_____,1975. Voluntary control and reactivity of human heart rate. *Psychophysiol.* **12**: 339–348.

Benson, H. 1975. *The relaxation response*. New York: William Morrow.

_____, B. A. Rosner, and B. R. Marzetta 1973. Decreased systolic blood pressure in hypertensive subjects who practiced meditation. *J. clin. Invest.* **52**: 8a.

_____, D. Shapiro, B. Tursky, and G. E. Schwartz 1971. Decreased systolic blood pressure through operant conditioning techniques in patients with essential hypertension. *Science* **173**: 740–742.

Berens, C., H. J. Girard, G. Fonda, and S.B. Sells 1957. Effects of tachistoscopic training on visual functions in myopic patients. *Am. J. Ophthal.* **44**: 25–48.

Berger, H. 1929. Uber das Elektrenkephalogramm des Menschen. *Arch. Psychiat. NervKrankh.* **87**: 527–570.

Bergman, J. S., and H. J. Johnson 1971. The effects of instructional set and autonomic perception on cardiac control. *Psychophysiol.* **8**: 180–190.

______ 1972. Sources of information which affect training and raising of heart rate. *Psychophysiol.* **9**: 30–39.

Bilodeau, E. A., and I. M. Bilodeau 1969. *Principles of skill acquisition.* New York: Academic Press.

Birk, L., A. Crider, D. Shapiro, and B. Tursky 1966. Operant electrodermal conditioning under partial curarization. *J. comp. physiol. Psychol.* **62**: 165–166.

Blanchard, E. B., and G. G. Abel 1976. An experimental case study of the biofeedback treatment of a rape-induced psychophysiological cardiovascular disorder. *Beh. Ther.* **7**: 113–119.

______, and L. H. Epstein 1977. Clinical applications of biofeedback. In M. Hersen, R. M. Eisler, and P. M. Miller (eds.), *Progress in behavior modification.* New York: Academic Press, Vol. IV.

______, and M. R. Haynes 1975. Biofeedback treatment of a case of Raynaud's disease. *J. beh. ther. and exp. Psychiat.* **6**: 230–234.

______, M. R. Haynes, M. D. Kallman, and L. Harkey 1976. A comparison of direct blood pressure feedback and electromyographic feedback on the blood pressure of normotensives. *Biofeedback and Self-Regulation* **1**: 445–451.

______, R. W. Scott, L. D. Young, and E. D. Edmundson 1974a. Effect of knowledge of response on the self-control of heart rate. *Psychophysiol.* **11**: 251–264.

______, R. W. Scott, L. D. Young, and M. R. Haynes 1974b. The effects of feedback signal information content on the long-term self-control of heart rate. *J. gen. Psychol.* **91**: 175–187.

______, and L. D. Young 1974. Clinical applications of biofeedback training: a review of evidence. *Arch. gen. Psychiat.* **30**: 530–589.

______, and L. D. Young 1972. Relative efficacy of visual and auditory feedback for self-control of heart rate. *J. gen. Psychol.* **87**: 195–202.

______, and L. D. Young 1973. Self-control of cardiac functioning: a promise as yet unfulfilled. *Psychol. Bull.* **79**: 145–163.

______, L. D. Young, and M. R. Haynes 1975. A simple feedback system for the treatment of elevated blood pressure. *Beh. Ther.* **6**: 241–245.

______, L. D. Young, M. R. Haynes, and M. D. Kallman 1974d. A simple feedback system for self-control of blood pressure. *Percept. Mot. Skills* **39**: 891–898.

______, L. D. Young, M. R. Haynes, and R. W. Scott 1975. Long-term instructional control of heart rate without exteroceptive feedback. *J. gen. Psychol.* **92**: 291–292.

______, L. D. Young, and P. McLeod 1972. Awareness of heart activity and control of heart rate. *Psychophysiol.* **9**: 63–68.

______, L. D. Young, R. W. Scott, and M. R. Haynes 1974c. Differential effects of feedback and reinforcement in voluntary acceleration of human heart rate. *Percept. Mot. Skills* **38**: 683–691.

Bleecker, E. R., and E. T. Engel 1973a. Learned control of ventricular rate in patients with atrial fibrillation. *Psychosom. Med.* **35**: 161–175.

______ 1973b. Learned control of cardiac rate and cardiac conduction in the Wolff-Parkinson-White syndrome. *New Eng. J. Med.* **288**: 560–562.

Booker, H. E., R. T. Rubow, and P. J. Coleman 1969. Simplified feedback in neuromuscular retraining: an automated approach using electromyographic signals. *Arch. Phys. Med. and Rehabil.* **50**: 621–625.

Bouchard, C., and J. A. Corson 1976. Heart rate regulation with success and failure signals. *Psychophysiol.* **13**: 69–74.

Boudewyns, P. A. 1976. A comparison of effects of stress vs relaxation instruction on the finger temperature response. *Beh. Ther.* **7**: 54–67.

Brener, J. 1974a. A general model of voluntary control applied to the phenomena of learned cardiovascular change. In P. A. Obrist, A. H. Black, J. Brener, and L. V. DiCara (eds.), *Cardiovascular psychophysiology.* Chicago: Aldine.

______ 1974b. Factors influencing the specificity of voluntary control. In L. V. DiCara (ed.), *Limbic and autonomic nervous system research.* Plenum.

______ 1974c. Summary. In P. A. Obrist, A. H. Black, J. Brener, and L. V. DiCara (eds.), *Cardiovascular psychophysiology*. Chicago: Aldine.

______ 1975. Learned control of cardiovascular processes: feedback mechanisms and therapeutic applications. In K. S. Calhoun, H. E. Adams, and K. M. Mitchell (eds.), *Innovative treatment methods in psychopathology*. New York: Wiley.

______, and D. Hothersall 1966. Heart rate control under conditions of augmented sensory feedback. *Psychophysiol.* **3**: 23–27.

______, and D. Hothersall 1967. Paced respiration and heart rate control. *Psychophysiol.* **4**: 1–6.

______, and J. M. Jones 1974. Interoceptive discrimination in intact humans: detection of cardiac activity. *Physiol. Beh.* **13**: 763–767.

______, and R. A. Kleinman 1970. Learned control of decreases in systolic blood pressure. *Nature* **226**: 1063–1064.

———, R. A. Kleinman, and W. J. Goesling 1969. The effects of different exposures to augmented sensory feedback on the control of heart rate. *Psychophysiol.* **5**: 510–516.

Brown, B. B. 1971. Awareness of EEG-subjective activity relationships detected within a closed feedback system. *Psychophysiol.* **7**: 451–464.

——— 1970. Recognition aspects of consciousness through association with EEG alpha activity represented by a light signal. *Psychophysiol.* **6**: 442–452.

Brudny, J., B. B. Grynbaum, and J. Korein 1974. Spasmodic torticollis: treatment by feedback display of the EMG. *Arch. Phys. Med. Rehabil.* **58**: 403–408.

———, J. Korein, B. B. Grynbaum, L. W. Friedmann, S. Weinstein, G. Sachs-Frankel, and P. V. Belandres 1976. EMG feedback therapy: review of treatment of 114 patients. *Arch. Phys. Med. Rehabil.* **57**: 55–61.

———, J. Korein, L. Levidow, B. B. Grynbaum, A. Lieberman, and L. W. Friedmann 1974. Sensory feedback therapy as a modality of treatment in central nervous system disorders of voluntary movement. *Neurology, Minneap.* **24**: 925–932.

Budzynski, T. H., and J. Stoyva 1973. An electromyographic feedback technique for teaching voluntary relaxation of the masseter muscle. *J. dent. Res.* **52**: 116–119.

——— 1969. An instrument for producing deep muscle relaxation by means of analogue information feedback. *J. appl. beh. Anal.* **2**: 231–237.

———, and C. S. Adler 1970. Feedback-influenced muscle relaxation: application to tension headache. *J. beh. Ther. exp. Psychiat.* **1**: 205–211.

———, C. S. Adler, and D. J. Mullaney 1973. EMG biofeedback and tension headache: a controlled outcome study. *Psychosom. Med.* **6**: 509–514.

Canter, A., C. Y. Kondo, and J. R. Knott 1975. A comparison of EMG feedback and progressive muscle relaxation training in anxiety neurosis. *Br. J. Psychiat.* **127**: 470–477.

Carlsöö, S., and A. K. Edfeldt 1963. Attempts at muscle control with visual and auditory impulses as auxiliary stimuli. *Scand. J. Psychol.* **4**: 231–235.

Carnahan, J. E., and C. A. Nugent 1975. The effects of self-monitoring by patients on the control of hypertension. *Am J. Med. Sci.* **269**: 69–73.

Chesney, M. A., and J. L. Shelton 1976. A comparison of muscle relaxation and electromyogram biofeedback treatments for muscle contraction headache. *J. beh. ther. exp. Psychiat.* **7**: 221–225.

Cleeland, C. S. 1973. Behavioral technics in the modification of spasmodic torticollis. *Neurology, Minneap.* **23**: 1241–1247.

Colgan, M. 1977. Effects of binary and proportional feedback on bidirectional control of heart rate. *Psychophysiol.* **14**: 187–191.

Collins, F. L., L. H. Epstein, and H. J. Hannay 1976. Modification of myopia using fading and reinforcement: a case study. Unpublished manuscript.

Cornsweet, T. N., and A. D. Crane 1973. Training the visual accommodative system. *Vision Res.* **13**: 713–715.

Coursey, R. D. 1975. Electromyograph feedback as a relaxation technique. *J. consult. clin. Psychol.* **43**: 825–834.

Cox, D. J., A. Freundlich, and R. G. Meyer 1975. Differential effectiveness of electromyograph feedback, verbal relaxation instructions, and medication placebo with tension headaches. *J. consult. clin. Psychol.* **43**: 892–899.

Danker, P. S., D. R. Niklich, C. Pratt, and T. L. Creer 1975. An unsuccessful attempt to instrumentally condition peak expiratory flow rates in asthmatic children. *J. psychosom. Res.* **19**: 209–213.

Davis, M. H., D. R. Saunders, T. L. Creer, and H. Chair 1973. Relaxation training facilitated by biofeedback apparatus as a supplemental treatment in bronchial asthma. *J. psychosom. Res.* **17**: 121–128.

Deckner, C. W., J. T. Hill, and J. R. Bourne 1972. Shaping of gastric motility in humans. *Proceedings 80th Annual Convention, APA*: 759–760.

DiCara, L.V., and N.E. Miller 1968a. Changes in heart rate instrumentally learned by curarized rats as avoidance responses. *J. comp. physiol. Psychol.* **65**: 8–12.

______ 1968b. Instrumental learning of systolic blood pressure responses by curarized rats: dissociation of cardiac and vascular changes. *Psychosom. Med.* **30**: 489–494.

______ 1968c. Instrumental learning of vasomotor responses by rats: learning to respond differentially in the two ears. *Science* **159**: 1485.

Elder, S. T., and N. K. Eustis 1975. Instrumental blood pressure conditioning in outpatient hypertensives. *Beh. Res. Ther.* **13**: 185–188.

______, Z. B. Ruiz, H. L. Deabler, R. L. Dillenkoffer 1973. Instrumental conditioning of diastolic blood pressure in essential hypertensive patients. *J. appl. beh. Anal.* **6**: 377–382.

Engel, B. T. 1972. Operant conditioning of cardiac function: a status report. *Psychophysiol.* **9**: 161–177.

______, and E. R. Bleecker 1974. Application of operant conditioning techniques to the control of cardiac arrhythmias. In P. A. Obrist, A. H. Black, J. Brener, and L. V. DiCara (eds.), *Cardiovascular psychophysiology.* Chicago: Aldine.

______, and R. A. Chism 1967. Operant conditioning of heart rate speeding. *Psychophysiol* 3: 418–426.

______, and S. P. Hansen 1966. Operant conditioning of heart rate slowing. *Psychophysiol.* 3: 176–187.

______, and L. Melmon 1968. Operant conditioning of heart rate in patients with cardiac arrhythmias. *Conditional Reflex* 3: 130.

______, P. Nikoomanesh, and M. M. Schuster 1974. Operant conditioning of rectosphincteric responses in the treatment of fecal incontinence. *New Engl. J. Med.* 290: 646–649.

Epstein, L. H., and G. G. Abel 1977. Analysis of biofeedback training effects for tension headache patients. *Beh. Ther.* 8: 37–47.

______, P. N. Cinciripini, J. F. McCoy, and W. R. Marshall 1977. Heart rate as a discriminative stimulus. *Psychophysiol.* 14: 143–149.

______, H. J. Hannay, and R. Looney 1975. *Fading and reinforcement in the modification of visual acuity.* Paper presented at the meeting of the Associations for the Advancement of Behavior Therapy, San Francisco, December.

______, M. Hersen, and D. P. Hemphill 1974. Music feedback in the treatment of tension headache: an experimental case study. *J. beh. Ther. and exp. Psychiat.* 5: 59–63.

______, D. R. Malone, and J. Cunningham 1976. *The use of sensory feedback training with stroke patients.* Paper presented at the annual meeting of the Alabama Society for Crippled Children and Adults, Mobile, October.

______, and D. Stein 1974. Feedback-influenced heart rate discrimination. *J. of abnorm. Psychol.* 83: 585–588.

______, and J. S. Webster 1975. Instructional, pacing, and feedback control of respiratory behavior. *Percept. Mot. Skills* 41: 895–900.

______, and J. S. Webster 1975. Reliability of various estimates of electromyogram activity: within and between subject analyses. *Psychophysiol.* 12: 468–470.

______, J. S. Webster, and G. G. Abel 1976. Self-managed relaxation in the treatment of tension headaches. In J. D. Krumboltz and C. E. Thoresen (eds.), *Counseling methods.* New York: Holt, Rinehart and Winston, pp. 344–348.

Feldman, G. M. 1976. The effect of biofeedback training on respiratory resistance of asthmatic children. *Psychosom. Med.* 38: 27–34.

Feuerstein, M., and H. A. Adams 1975. *Cephalic vasomotor feedback with a treatment of migraine headache: an alternative therapeutic approach.* Paper presented at the Association for Advancement of Behavior Therapy, San Francisco.

Fey, S. G., and E. Lindholm 1975. Systolic blood pressure and heart rate changes during three sessions involving biofeedback or no feedback. *Psychophysiol.* **12**: 513–519.

Finley, W. W. 1976. Effects of sham feedback following successful SMR training in an epileptic: follow-up study. *Biofeedback and Self-Regulation* **1**: 227–235.

______ 1970. The effect of feedback on the control of cardiac rate. *J. Psychol.* **77**: 43–54.

______, H. A. Smith, and M. D. Etherton 1975. Reduction of seizures and normalization of the EEG in a severe epileptic following sensorimotor biofeedback training. *Biological Psychol.* **2**: 195–209.

Fleishman, E. A. 1966. Human abilities and the acquisition of skill. In E. A. Bilodeau (ed.), *Acquisition of skill*. New York: Academic Press.

Frazier, T. W. 1966. Avoidance conditioning of heart rate in humans. *Psychophysiol.* **3**: 188–202.

Friar, L. R., and J. Beatty 1976. Migraine: management by a trained control of vasoconstriction. *J. consult. clin. Psychol.* **44**: 46–53.

Fruhling, M., J. V. Basmajian, and T. G. Simard 1969. A note on the conscious controls of motor units by children under six. *J. mot. Beh.* **1**: 65–68.

Furman, S. 1973. Intestinal biofeedback in functional diarrhea: a preliminary report. *J. beh. Ther. exp. Psychiat.* **4**: 317–321.

Gannon, L., and R. A. Sternbach 1971. Alpha enhancement as a treatment for pain: a case study. *J. beh. Ther. exp. Psychiat.* **2**: 209–213.

Gardner, E. P., and F. J. Keefe 1976. *Effects of knowledge of response on temperature biofeedback training.* Paper presented at meeting of Biofeedback Research Society, Colorado Springs.

Gatchel, R. J. 1975. Change over training sessions of relationship between locus of control and voluntary heart-rate control. *Percept. Mot. Skills* **40**: 424–426.

______ 1974. Frequency of feedback and learned heart rate control. *J. exp. Psychol.* **103**: 274–283.

Gavalas, R. J. 1968. Operant reinforcement of a skeletally mediated autonomic response: uncoupling of the two responses. *Psychonomic Sci.* **11**: 195–196.

Giddings, J. W., and R. I. Lanyon 1974. Effects of reinforcement of visual acuity in myopic adults. *Amer. J. Optom. physiol. Optics* **51**: 181–188.

Gleuck, B. C., and C. F. Stroebel 1975. Biofeedback and meditation in the treatment of psychiatric illnesses. *Comprehensive Psychiat.* **16**: 303–321.

Green, E. E., E. D. Walters, A. M. Green, and G. Murphy 1969. Feedback technique for deep relaxation. *Psychophysiol.* **6**: 371–377.

Greene, W. A. 1976. Operant conditioning of the GSR using partial reinforcement. *Psychol. Rep.* **19**: 571–578.

Guenther, C. R., and R. A. McFarland 1973. Effect of motivation upon performance of an operant heart rate control task. *Psychol. Rep.* **32**: 659–663.

Guitar, B. 1975. Reduction of stuttering frequency using analogue electromyographic feedback. *J. Speech Hear. Res.* **18**: 672–685.

Guyton, A. C. 1961. *Textbook of medical physiology.* (2nd ed.) Philadelphia: Saunders.

Haines, R. W. 1932. The laws of muscle and tendon growth. *J. Anat.* **66**: 578–585.

______ 1934. On muscles of full and of short action. *J. Anat.* **69**: 20–24.

Hardyck, C. D., and L. F. Petrinovich 1969. Treatment of subvocal speech during reading. *J. Reading* **1**: 3–11.

______, and D. W. Ellsworth 1966. Feedback of speech muscle activity during silent reading: rapid extinction. *Science* **154**: 1467–1468.

Harris, V. A., E. S. Katkin, J. R. Lick, and T. Habberfield 1976. Paced respiration as a technique for the modification of autonomic response to stress. *Psychophysiol.* **13**: 386–391.

Harrison, V. F., and O. A. Mortensen 1962. Identification and voluntary control of single motor unit activity in the tibialis anterior muscle. *Anat. Rec.* **144**: 109–116.

Hart, J. T. 1967. *Autocontrol of EEG alpha.* Paper presented at meeting of Society for Psychophysiological Research, San Diego, October.

Haynes, S. N., P. Griffin, D. Mooney, and M. Parise 1975. Electromyographic biofeedback and relaxation instructions in the treatment of muscle contraction headaches. *Beh. Ther.* **6**: 672–678.

______, D. Moseley, and W. T. McGowan 1974. Relaxation training and biofeedback in the reduction of muscle tension. *Psychophysiol.* **12**: 547–553.

Headrick, M. W., B. W. Feather, and D. T. Wells 1971. Unidirectional and large magnitude heart rate changes with augmented sensory feedback. *Psychophysiol.* **8**: 132–142.

Hefferline, R. F., B. Keenan, and R. A. Hanford 1959. Escape and avoidance conditioning in human subjects without their observation of the response. *Science* **130**: 1338–1339.

______, and T. B. Perera 1963. Proprioceptive discrimination of a covert operant without its observation by the subject. *Science* **139**: 834–835.

Henson, D. E., and H. B. Rubin 1971. Voluntary control of eroticism. *J. appl. beh. Anal.* **4**: 37–44.

Herman, S. H., and M. Prewett 1974. An experimental analysis of feedback to increase sexual arousal in a case of homo- and heterosexual impotence: a preliminary report. *J. beh. Ther. exp. Psychiat.* **5**: 271–274.

Hersen, M. 1973. Self-assessment of fear. *Beh. Ther.* **4**: 241–257.

______, and D. H. Barlow 1976. *Single-case experimental designs: strategies for studying behavior change.* New York: Pergamon.

Hnatiow, M. 1971. Learned control of heart rate and blood pressure. *Percept. Mot. Skills* **33**: 219–220.

______, and P. J. Lang 1965. Learned stabilization of cardiac rate. *Psychophysiol.* **1**: 330–336.

Jacobs, A., and G. S. Felton 1969. Visual feedback of myoelectric output to facilitate muscle relaxation in normal persons and patients with neck injuries. *Archs. Phys. Med. Rehabil.* **50**: 34–39.

Jacobson, A. M., T. P. Hackett, O. S. Surman, and E. L. Silverberge 1973. Raynaud's phenomenon: treatment with hypnotic and operant technique. *J.A.M.A.* **225**: 739–740.

Jacobson, E. 1976. *You must relax.* (5th ed.) New York: McGraw-Hill.

James, W. 1890. *Principles of psychology.* New York: Holt.

Johns, T. R. 1970. *Heart rate control in humans under paced respiration and restricted movement: the effect of instructions and exteroceptive feedback.* Unpublished doctoral dissertation, University of Miami (Florida).

Johnson, C. P. 1976. Analysis of five tests commonly used in determining the ability to control single motor units. *Am. J. phys. Med.* **55**: 113–121.

Johnson, H. E., and W. H. Garton 1973. Muscle reeducation in hemiplegia by use of electromyographic device. *Archs. phys. Med. Rehabil.* **54**: 320–325.

Johnson, R. K., and R. G. Meyer 1974. Phases biofeedback approach for epileptic seizure control. *J. beh. Ther. exp. Psychiat.* **5**: 185–187.

Jones, F. W., and B. S. Holmes 1976. Alcoholism, alpha production, and biofeedback. *J. consult. clinical Psychol.* **44**: 224–228.

Kamiya, J. 1962. *Conditioned discrimination of the EEG alpha rhythm in humans.* Paper presented at the Western Psychological Association, San Francisco.

______ 1968. Conscious control of brain waves. *Psychol. Today* **1**, (1): 57–60.

Kaplan, B. J. 1975. Biofeedback in epileptics: equivocal relationship of reinforced EEG frequency to seizure reduction. *Epilepsia* **16**: 477–485.

Katkin, E., and E. N. Murray 1968. Instrumental conditioning of autonomically mediated behavior: theoretical and methodological issues. *Psychol. Bull.* **70**: 52–68.

Kazdin, A. E. 1974. Self-monitoring and behavior change. In M. J. Mahoney and E. F. Thoresen (eds.), *Self-control: power to the person.* Monterey: Brooks/Cole, pp. 218–246.

Keefe, F. J. 1975. Conditioning changes in differential skin temperature. *Percept. Mot. Skills* **40**: 283–288.

Kimble, G. A. 1961. *Hilgard and Marquis' conditioning and learning.* New York: Appleton-Century-Crofts.

Kimmel, H. D. 1967. Instrumental conditioning of autonomically mediated behavior. *Psychol. Bull.* **67**: 337–345.

——— 1974. Instrumental conditioning of autonomically mediated responses. *Am. Psychol.* **29**: 325–335.

———, and F. A. Hill 1960. Operant conditioning of the GSR. *Psychol. Rep.* **7**: 555–562.

Kinsman, R. A., K. O'Banion, S. Robinson, and H. Staudenmayer 1975. Continuous biofeedback and discrete posttrial verbal feedback in frontalis muscle relaxation training. *Psychophysiol.* **12**: 30–35.

Koppman, J.W., R.D. McDonald, and N.G. Kunzel 1974. Voluntary regulation of temporal artery diameter by migraine patients. *Headache* **10**: 133–138.

Kristt, D. A., and B. T. Engel 1975. Learned control of blood pressure in patients with high blood pressure. *Circulation* **51**: 370–378.

Kukulka, C. G., and J. V. Basmajian 1975. Assessment of an audiovisual feedback device used in motor training. *Am. J. phys. Med.* **54**: 194–208.

Kurtz, P. S. 1974. Treating chemical dependency through biofeedback. *Hos. Prog.* **55**: 68–69.

Lamontagne, Y., I. Hand, L. Annable, and M. Gagnon 1975. Physiological and psychological effects of alpha and EMG feedback training with college drug users: a pilot study. *Can. Psychiart. Ass. J.* **20**: 337–349.

Lang, P. J. 1975. Acquisition of heart-rate control: method, theory, and clinical implications. In D. C. Fowles (ed.), *Clinical applications of psychophysiology.* New York: Columbia University Press.

———, 1968. Fear reduction and fear behavior: problems in treating a construct. In J. M. Shlien (ed.), *Research in psychotherapy:* Vol. III. Washington, D. C.: American Psychological Association.

______ 1974. Learned control of human heart rate in a computer directed environment. In P. A. Obrist, A. H. Black, J. Brener, and L. V. DiCara (eds.), *Cardiovascular psychophysiology,* New York: Aldine.

______ 1969. The mechanics of desensitization and the laboratory study of human fear. In C. M. Franks (ed.), *Behavior therapy: appraisal and status.* New York: McGraw-Hill.

______, L. A. Sroufe, and J. E. Hastings 1967. Effects of feedback and instructional set on the control of cardiac rate variability. *J. exp. Psychol.* **75:** 425–431.

______, W. G. Troyer, C. T. Twentyman, and R. J. Gatchel 1975. Differential effects of heart rate modification training on college students, older males, and patients with ischemic heart disease. *Psychosom. Med.* **37:** 429–446.

______, and C. T. Twentyman 1974. Learning to control heart rate: binary vs analogue feedback. *Psychophysiol.* **11:** 616–629.

______, and C. T. Twentyman 1976. Learning to control heart rate: effects of varying incentive and criterion of success on past performance. *Psychophysiol.* **13:** 378–385.

Lanyon, R. I., C. C. Barrington, and A. C. Newman 1976. Modification of stuttering through EMG biofeedback: A preliminary study. *Beh. Ther.* **7:** 96–103.

Laws, D. R. and H. B. Rubin 1969. Instructional control of an automatic sexual response. *J. appl. beh. Anal.* **2:** 93–99.

Leaf, W. B., and K. R. Gaarder 1971. A simplified electromyograph feedback apparatus for relaxation training. *J. beh. Ther. exp. Psychiat.* **2:** 39–43.

Leibrecht, B. C., A. J. Lloyd, and S. Pounder 1973. Auditory feedback and conditioning of the single motor unit. *Psychophysiol.* **10:** 1–7.

Leitenberg, H., W. S. Agras, R. Butz, and J. Wincze 1971. Relationship between heart rate and behavior change during the treatment of phobias. *J. abnorm. Psychol.* **78:** 59–68.

Levene, H. I., B. T. Engel, and J. A. Pearson 1968. Differential operant conditioning of heart rate. *Psychosom. Med.* **30:** 837–845.

Levenson, R. W. 1974. Automated system for direct measurement and feedback of total respiratory resistance by the forced oscillation technique. *Psychophysiol.* **11:** 86–90.

______ 1976. Feedback effects and respiratory involvement in voluntary control of heart rate. *Psychophysiol.* **13:** 108–114.

______, S. B. Manuck, H. H. Strupp, G. L. Blackwood, and J. D. Snell 1974. *A biofeedback technique for bronchial asthma.* Paper presented to the annual meeting of the Biofeedback Research Society, Colorado Springs, February.

———, and H. H. Strupp 1972. *Simultaneous feedback in control of heart rate and respiration rate.* Paper presented at 12th Annual meeting of the Society for Psychophysiological Research, November.

Lindsley, D. B. 1935. Electrical activity of human motor units during voluntary contraction. *Am J. Physiol.* **114**: 90–99.

Lloyd, A. J., and B. C. Leibrecht 1971. Conditioning of a single motor unit. *J. exp. Psychol.* **88**: 391–395.

———, and T.J. Shurley 1976. The effects of sensory perceptual isolation on single motor unit conditioning. *Psychophysiol.* **13**: 340–344.

Love, W. A., D. D. Montgomery, and T. A. Moeller 1974. Working paper number 1. Unpublished manuscript. Nova University, Ft. Lauderdale.

Lubar, J. F., and W. W. Bahler 1976. Behavioral management of epileptic seizures following EEG biofeedback training of the sensorimotor rhythm. *Biofeedback and Self-Regulation* **1**: 77–104.

Lutker, E. R. 1971. Treatment of migraine headache by conditioned relaxation: a case study. *Beh. Ther.* **2**: 592–593.

Lynch, W. C., H. Hama, S. Kohn, and N. E. Miller 1976. Instrumental control of peripheral vasomotor responses in children. *Psychophisiol.* **13**: 219–221.

——— 1974. *Instrumental learning of vasomotor responses: a progress report.* Paper presented at meeting of the Biofeedback Research Society, Colorado, Springs.

Malmo, R. B., and C. Shagass 1949. Physiologic study of symptom mechanisms in psychiatric patients under stress. *Psychosom. Med.* **11**: 25–29.

———, and F. H. Davis 1950. Symptom specificity and bodily reactions during psychiatric interview. *Psychosom. Med.* **12**: 362–276.

Malmstrom, F. V., and R. J. Rundle 1976. Effects of visual imagery on the accommodation response. *Percept. and Psychophys.* **19**: 450–453.

Mandler, G., J. M. Mandler, and E. T. Uviller 1958. Autonomic feedback: the perception of autonomic activity. *J. abnorm. Soc. Psychol.* **58**: 367–373.

Manuck, S. B., R. W. Levenson, J. J. Henricksen, and S. L. Gryll 1975. Role of feedback in voluntary control of heart rate. *Percept. mot. skills* **40**: 747–752.

Marinacci, A. A., and M. Horande 1960. Electromyogram in neuromuscular reeducation. *Bull. Los Ang. neurol. Soc.* **25**: 57–71.

Martin, J. E., and L. H. Epstein 1976. *Self-monitoring of physiological responses.* Paper presented at the annual meeting of the Association for the Advancement of Behavior Therapy, New York, December.

Maslach, C., G. Marshall, and B. G. Zimbardo 1972. Hypnotic control of peripheral skin temperature: a case report. *Psychophysiol.* **9**: 600–605.

Matthews, A. M., and M. G. Gelder 1969. Psychophysiological investigations of brief relaxation training. *J. Psyhosom. Res.* **13**: 1–12.

May, D. S., and C. A. Weber 1976. *Temperature feedback training with a symptom reduction in Raynaud's disease: a controlled study.* Paper presented to 7th Annual Meeting of Biofeedback Research Society, Colorado Springs, February.

May, J. R., and H. J. Johnson 1972. *Operant of conditioning with human heart rate decreases and schedules of reinforcement.* Paper presented to annual meeting of Western Psychological Association, Portland.

McFarland, R. A. 1975. Heart rate and heart rate control. *Psychophysiol.* **12**: 402–405.

McGuigan, F. J. 1967. Feedback of speech muscle activity during silent reading: two comments. *Science* **157**: 579–580.

McKenzie, R. E., W. J. Ehrisman, P. S. Montgomery, and R. H. Barnes 1974. The treatment of headache by means of electroencephalographic biofeedback. *Headache* **14**: 164–172.

Melzack, R., and C. Perry 1975. Self-regulation of pain: the use of alpha-feedback and hypnotic training for the control of chronic pain. *Exp. Neurol.* **46**: 452–469.

Miller, N. E. 1969. Learning of visceral and glandular responses. *Science* **163**: 434–445.

______ 1972. Postscript. In D. Singh and C. T. Morgan (eds.), *Current status of physiological psychology: readings.* Montery, Calif.: Brooks-Cole. 1972.

______, L. V. DiCara, V. H. Solomon, J. M. Weiss, and B. R. Dworkin 1970. Learned modifications of autonomic functions: a review and some new data. *Circulation Res.* **36**, (Supplement 1: 3–11).

______, and B. R. Dworkin 1974. Visceral learning: recent difficulties with curarized rats and significant problems for human research. In D. A. Obrist *et al.* (eds.), *Cardiovascular psychophysiology*, Chicago: Aldine, p. 312–331.

Mills, G. K., and L. Solyom 1974. Biofeedback of EEG alpha in the treatment of obsessive ruminations: an exploration. *J. beh. Ther. exp. Psychiat.* **5**: 37–41.

Mitchell, K R., and D. M. Mitchell 1971. Migraine: an exploratory treatment application of programmed behavior therapy techniques. *J. Psychosom. Res.* **15**: 137–157.

Mulholland, T. 1968. Feedback electroencephalography. *Activitas nerv. Sup. Prague,* **10**: 410–438.

——— 1973. Objective EEG methods for studying covert shifts of visual attention. In F. J. McGuigan (ed.), *The psychophysiology of thinking.* New York: Academic Press, pp. 109–151.

———, and E. Peper 1971. Occipital alpha and accommodative vergence, pursuit tracking, and fast eye movements. *Psychophysiol.* **8**: 556–575.

Netsell, R., and C. S. Cleeland 1973. Modification of lip hypertonia in dysarthria using EMG feedback. *J. Speech Hear. Disorders* **38**: 131–140.

Nikoomanesh, P., D. Wells, and M. M. Schuster 1973. Biofeedback control of lower esophageal sphincter contraction. *Clin. Res.* **21**: 521.

Nowlis, D. P., and J. Kamiya 1970. The control of electroencephalographic alpha rhythms through auditory feedback and the associated mental activity. *Psychophysiol.* **6**: 476–484.

Nunes, J. S., and I. M. Marks 1975. Feedback of true heart rate during exposure in vivo. *Arch. gen. Psychiat.* **32**: 933–936.

Obrist, P. A. 1976. The cardiovascular-behavioral interaction—as it appears today. *Psychophysiol.* **13**: 95–107.

———, R. A. Galosy, J. E. Lawler, C. H. Gaebelein, J. L. Howard, and E. M. Shanks 1975. Operant conditioning of heart rate: somatic correlates. *Psychophysiol.* **12**: 445–455.

Paskewitz, D. A., and M. T. Orne 1973. Visual effects on alpha feedback training. *Science.* **181**: 360–363.

Patel, C. H. 1973. Yoga and biofeedback in the management of hypertension. *Lancet* ii: 1053–1055.

——— 1975. 12-month follow-up of yoga and biofeedback in the management of hypertension. *Lancet* i: 62–67.

———, and W. R. S. North 1975. Randomized controlled trial of yoga and biofeedback in management of hypertension. *Lancet* ii: 93–99.

Peper, E. 1970. Feedback regulation of the alpha electroencephalogram activity through control of the internal and external parameters. *Kybernetic* **7**: 107–112.

Petajan, J. H., and B. A. Philip 1969. Frequency control of motor unit action potentials. *Electroenceph. clin. Neurophysiol.* **27**: 66–72.

Pickering, T., and G. Gorham 1975. Learned heart-rate controlled by a patient with a ventricular parasystolic rhythm. *Lancet,* February 1: 252–253.

Plotkin, W. B. 1976. On the self-regulation of the occipital alpha rhythm: control strategies, states of consciousness, and the role of physiological feedback. *J. exp. Psychol. gen.* **105**: 66–99.

Price, K. R. 1973. *Feedback effects on penile tumescence.* Paper presented to Eastern Psychological Association, Washington, May.

Prigatano, G. P., and H. J. Johnson 1972. Biofeedback control of heart rate variability to phobic stimuli: a new approach to treating spider phobia. In *Proceedings of Annual Convention, APA.* Washington: American Psychological Association, pp. 403–404.

______ 1974. Autonomic nervous system changes associated with spider phobic reaction. *J. abnorm. Psychol.* **83**: 169–177.

Provine, R. R., and J. M. Enoch 1975. On voluntary ocular accommodation. *Percept. Psychophys.* **17**: 209–212.

Raskin, M., G. Johnson, and J. W. Rondestvedt 1973. Chronic anxiety treated by feedback-induced muscle relaxation. *Arch. gen. Psychiat.* **28**: 263–267.

Ray, W. J. 1974. The relationship of locus of control, self-report measures, and feedback to the voluntary control of heart rate. *Psychophysiol.* **11**: 527–534.

______, and S. B. Lamb 1974. Locus of control and the voluntary control of heart rate. *Psychosom. Med.* **36**: 180–182.

Reinking, R. H., and M. L. Kohl 1975. Effects of various forms of relaxation training on physiological and self-report measures of relaxation. *J. consult. clin. Psychol.* **43**: 595–600.

Rice, D. G. 1966. Operant conditioning and associated electromyogram responses. *J. exp. Psychol.* **163**: 434–445.

Roberts, A. H., D. G. Kewman, and H. MacDonald 1973. Voluntary control of skin temperature: unilateral changes using hypnosis in feedback. *J. abnorm. Psychol.* **82**: 163–168.

Rosen, R. C. 1973. Suppression of penile tumescence by instrumental conditioning. *Psychosom. Med.* **35**: 509–513.

______ 1974. *The control of penile tumescence in the human male.* Paper presented to American Psychological Association, New Orleans.

Rotter, J. D. 1966. Generalized expectancies for internal vs external control of reinforcement. *Psychol. Monogr.* **80** (Whole No. 609): 1–28.

Rouse, L., J. Peterson, and G. Shapiro 1974. *EEG alpha entrainment reaction within the biofeedback setting and some possible effects on epilepsy.* Paper presented to Biofeedback Research Society meeting, February, Colorado Springs.

Rubow, R. T., and K. U. Smith 1971. Feedback parameters of electromyographic learning. *Amer. J. Phys. Med.* **50**: 115–131.

Russ, K. L. 1974. *Effect of two different feedback paradigms on blood pressure levels of patients with essential hypertension.* Paper presented to Biofeedback Research Society Meeting, February, Colorado Springs.

Sargent, J. D., E. E. Green, and E. D. Walters 1972. The use of autogenic feedback training in a pilot study of migraine and tension headaches. *Headache* **12**: 120–125.

——— 1973. Preliminary report on the use of autogenic feedback training in the treatment of migraine and tension headaches. *Psychosom. Med.* **35**: 129–135.

Schacter, S. 1971. *Emotion, obesity, and crime.* New York: Academic.

Schandler, S. L. and W. W. Grings 1976. An examination of methods for producing relaxation during short-term laboratory sessions. *Beh. Res. Ther.* **14**: 419–426.

Schultz, J. H., and W. Luthe 1969. *Autogenic training.* (Vol I.) New York: Grune and Stratton.

Schwartz, G. E. 1972a. Voluntary control of human cardiovascular integration and differentiation in man through feedback and reward. *Science* **175**: 90–93.

——— 1972b. Clinical applications of biofeedback: some theoretical issues. In D. Upper and D. S. Goodenough (eds.), *Behavior modification with the individual patient: Proceedings of Third Annual Brockton Symposium on Behavior Therapy.* Nutley, N. J.: Roche.

——— 1974. Toward a theory of voluntary control of response patterns in the cardiovascular system. In P. A. Obrist, A. H. Black, J. Brener, and L. V. DiCara (eds.), *Cardiovascular psychophysiology.* Chicago: Aldine.

——— 1975. Biofeedback, self-regulation, and the patterning of physiological processes. *Am. Scient.* **63**: 314–324.

———, and D. Shapiro 1973. Biofeedback and essential hypertension: current findings and theoretical concerns. In L. Birk (ed.), *Biofeedback: behavioral medicine.* New York: Grune and Stratton.

———, D. Shapiro, and B. Tursky 1971. Learned control of cardiovascular integration in man through operant conditioning. *Psychosom. Med.* **33**: 57–62.

Scott, R. W., R. D. Peters, W. J. Gillespie, E. B. Blanchard, E. D. Edmundson, and L. D. Young 1973a. The use of shaping and reinforcement in the operant acceleration and deceleration of heart rate. *Beh. Res. Ther.* **11**: 179–185.

______, E. B. Blanchard, E. D. Edmundson, and L. D. Young 1973b. A shaping procedure for heart-rate control in chronic tachycardia. *Percept. Mot. Skills* **37**: 327–338.

Scully, H. E., and J. V. Basmajian 1969. Motor-unit training and influence of manual skill. *Psychophysiol.* **5**: 625–632.

Sedlacek, K. 1976. *EMG and thermal feedback for treatment of Raynaud's disease.* Paper presented to 7th Annual Meeting of Biofeedback Research Society, Colorado Springs, February.

Seifert, A. R., and J. F. Lubar 1975. Reduction of epileptic seizures through EEG biofeedback training. *Biol. Psychol.* **3**: 157–184.

Shapiro, D. 1974. Operant-feedback control of human blood pressure: some clinical issues. In P. A. Obrist, A. H. Balck, J. Brener, and L. V. DiCara (eds.), *Cardiovascular psychophysiology.* Chicago: Aldine.

______, G. E. Schwartz, and B. Tursky 1972. Control of diastolic blood pressure in man by feedback and reinforcement. *Psychophysiol.* **9**: 296–304.

______, B. Tursky, E. Gershon, and M. Stern, 1969. Effects of feedback and reinforcement on control of human systolic blood pressure. *Science* **163**: 558–590.

______, B. Tursky, and G. E. Schwartz 1970a. Differentiation of heart rate and systolic blood pressure in man by operant conditioning. *Psychosom. Med.* **32**: 417–423.

______, B. Tursky, and G. E. Schwartz 1970b. Control of blood pressure in man by operant conditioning. *Circulation Res.* **26**, (Suppl. 1: 27–32).

Shaw, J. C. 1967. Quantification of biological signals using integration techniques. In P. H. Venables and I. Martin (eds.), *Manual of psychophysiological methods.* New York: Wiley pp. 404–465.

Shearn, D. W. 1962. Operant conditioning of heart rate. *Science* **137**: 530–531.

Shoemaker, J. E., and D. L. Tasto 1975. The effects of muscle relaxation on blood pressure of essential hypertensives. *Beh. Res. Ther.* **13**: 29–43.

Shrum, A. W. F. 1967. A study of the speaking behavior of stutterers and nonstutterers by means of multichannel electromyography. *Diss. Abstr.* **26**, (2-A): 825.

Simard, T. G. 1969. Fine sensorimotor control in healthy children: an electromyographic study. *Pediatrics* **43**: 1035–1041.

______, and J. V. Basmajian 1967. Methods in training the conscious control of motor units. *Arch. phys. Med. Rehabil.* **48**: 12–19.

Sirota, A. D., G. E. Schwartz, and D. Shapiro. Voluntary control of human heart rate: effect on reaction to aversive stimulation. *J. abnorm. Psychol.* **83**: 261–267.

Snyder, C., and M. Noble 1968. Operant conditioning of vasoconstriction. *J. exp. Psychol.* **77**: 263–268.

Sroufe, L. A. 1969. Learned stabilization of cardiac rate with respiration experimentally controlled. *J. exp. Psychol.* **81**: 391–393.

——— 1971. Effects of depth and rate of breathing on heart rate and heart rate variability. *Psychophysiol.* **8**: 648–655.

Stephens, J. H., A. H. Harris, and J. V. Brady 1972. Large magnitude heart rate changes in subjects instructed to change their heart rates and given exteroceptive feedback. *Psychophysiol.* **9**: 283–285.

———, and J. W. Shaffer 1975. Psychological and physiological variables associated with large magnitude voluntary heart rate changes. *Psychophysiol.* **12**: 381–387.

Sterman, M. B. Neurophysiological and clinical studies of sensorimotor EEG biofeedback training: some effects on epilepsey. In L. Birk (ed.), *Biofeedback: behavioral medicine.* New York: Grune and Stratton.

———, and L. Friar 1972. Suppression of seizures in an epileptic following sensorimotor EEG feedback training. *Electroenceph. clin. Neurophysiol.* **33**: 89–95.

———, L. R. MacDonald, and R. K. Stone 1974. Biofeedback training of the sensorimotor electroencephalograph in man: effects on epilepsy. *Epilepsia* **15**: 395–416.

Stern, R. N., and R. P. Pavloski 1974. Operant conditioning of vasoconstriction: a verification. *J. exp. Psychol.* **102**: 330–332.

Stoyva, J., and T. Budzynski 1974. Cultivated low arousal: an antistress response? In L. DiCara (ed.), *Limbic and autonomic nervous system research.* New York: Plenum.

Surwit, R. S. 1973. Biofeedback: A possible treatment for Raynaud's disease. In L. Birk (ed.), *Biofeedback: behavioral medicine.* New York: Grune and Stratton.

———, D. Shapiro, and J. L. Feld 1976. Digital temperature autoregulation and associated cardiovascular changes. *Psychophysiol.* **13**: 242–248.

Swann, D., P. C. W. van Wieringen, and D. Fokkema, 1974. Auditory electromyographic feedback therapy to inhibit undesired motor activity. *Arch. phys. Med. Reh.* **55**: 251–254.

Tasto, D. L., and J. E. Hinkle 1973. Muscle relaxation treatment for tension headaches. *Beh. Res. Ther.* **11**: 347–349.

Taub, E., and C. E. Emurian 1973. Autoregulation of skin temperature using a variable intensity light. In D. Shapiro *et al., (eds.), Biofeedback and self-control.* Chicago: Aldine, p. 504 (Abstract).

Teng, E. L., D. R. McNeal, N. Krajl, and R. L. Waters 1976. Electrical stimulation and feedback training: effects on the voluntary control of paretic muscles. *Arch. phys. Med. Rehabil.* **57**: 228–233.

Thoresen, C. E., and M. J. Mahoney 1974. *Behavioral self-control.* New York: Holt, Rinehart and Winston.

Townsend, R. E., J. F. House, and D. Addario 1975. A comparison of biofeedback-mediated relaxation and group therapy in the treatment of chronic anxiety. *Am. J. Psychiat.* **132**: 598–601.

Trowill, J. A. 1967. Instrumental conditioning of the heart rate in the curarized rat. *J. comp. physiol. Psychol.* **63**: 7–11.

Turin, A., and W. G. Johnson 1976. Biofeedback therapy for migraine headaches. *Arch. gen. Psychiat.* **33**: 517–519.

Tursky, B., D. Shapiro, and G. E. Schwartz 1972. Automated constant cuff-pressure system to measure average systolic and diastolic blood pressure in man. *IEEE Transactions in Bio-Medical Engineering* **19**: 217–276.

Vachon, L., and E. S. Rich 1976. Visceral learning in asthma. *Psychosom. Med.* **38**: 122–130.

Wagman, I. H., D. S. Pierce, and R. E. Burger 1965. Proprioceptive influence in volitional control of individual motor units. *Nature* **207**: 957–958.

Walsh, D. H. 1974. Interactive effects of alpha feedback and instructional set on subjective state. *Psychophysiol.* **11**: 428–435.

Weiss, T., and B. T. Engel 1970. Voluntary control of premature ventricular contractions in patients. *Am. J. Cardiol.* **26**: 666.

______ 1971. Operant conditioning of heart rate in patients with premature ventricular contractions. *Psychosom. Med.* **33**: 301–321.

______ 1975. Evaluation of an intracardiac limit of learned heart rate control. *Psychophysiol* **12**: 310–312.

Welgan, P. R. 1974. Learned control of gastric acid secretions in ulcer patients. *Psychosom. Med.* **36**: 411–419.

Wells, D. T. 1973 Large magnitude voluntary heart rate changes. *Psychophysiol.* **10**: 260–269.

Welsh, D. M., S. T. Elder, A. Longacre, and R. McAfee 1977. Acquisition, discrimative stimulus control, and tension of increases/decreases in blood pressure of normotensive human subjects. *J. appl. beh. anal.* in press.

Whitehead, W. E., P. F. Renault, and I. Goldiamond 1975. Modification of human gastric acid secretion with operant-conditioning procedures. *J appl. beh. Anal.* **8**: 147–156.

Wickramasekera, I. 1973b. The application of verbal instructions and EMG feedback training to the management of tension headache: preliminary observations. *Headache* 13: 74–76.

______ 1973a. Temperature feedback for the control of migraine. *J. beh. Ther. exp. Psychiat.* 4: 343–345.

______ 1974. Heart rate feedback and the management of cardiac neurosis. *J. abnorm. Psychol.* 83: 578–580.

Williams, D. E. 1955. Masseter muscle action potentials in stuttered and nonstuttered speech. *J. Speech Hear. Disorders.* 20: 242–261.

Wolff, H. G. 1963. *Headache and other pain.* New York: Oxford University Press.

Wolpe, J., and A. A. Lazarus, 1966. *Behavior therapy techniques.* Oxford: Pergamon.

Young, L. D., and E. B. Blanchard, 1974. Effects of auditory feedback of varying information content on the self-control of heart rate. *J. gen. Psychol.* 91: 61–68.

Zappalá, A. 1970. Influence of training and sex on the isolation and control of single motor units. *Am. J. Phys. Med.* 49: 348–361.

Zuckerman, M. 1971. Physiological measures of sexual arousal in the human. *Psychol. Bull.* 75: 279–329.

Index